Cambridge Elements

Elements in Historical Theory and Practice
edited by
Daniel Woolf
Queen's University, Ontario

THE HISTORY OF CONTINGENCY AND FUTURE-ORIENTED THOUGHT

Thomas Moynihan
Cambridge University

Shaftesbury Road, Cambridge CB2 8EA, United Kingdom

One Liberty Plaza, 20th Floor, New York, NY 10006, USA

477 Williamstown Road, Port Melbourne, VIC 3207, Australia

314–321, 3rd Floor, Plot 3, Splendor Forum, Jasola District Centre, New Delhi – 110025, India

Cambridge University Press is part of Cambridge University Press & Assessment, a department of the University of Cambridge.

We share the University's mission to contribute to society through the pursuit of education, learning and research at the highest international levels of excellence.

www.cambridge.org
Information on this title: www.cambridge.org/9781009571616

DOI: 10.1017/9781009358767

© Thomas Moynihan 2026

This publication is in copyright. Subject to statutory exception and to the provisions of relevant collective licensing agreements, no reproduction of any part may take place without the written permission of Cambridge University Press & Assessment.

When citing this work, please include a reference to the DOI 10.1017/9781009358767

First published 2026

A catalogue record for this publication is available from the British Library

A Cataloging-in-Publication data record for this Element is available from the Library of Congress

ISBN 978-1-009-57161-6 Hardback
ISBN 978-1-009-35878-1 Paperback
ISSN 2634-8616 (online)
ISSN 2634-8608 (print)

Cambridge University Press & Assessment has no responsibility for the persistence or accuracy of URLs for external or third-party internet websites referred to in this publication and does not guarantee that any content on such websites is, or will remain, accurate or appropriate.

For EU product safety concerns, contact us at Calle de José Abascal, 56, 1°, 28003 Madrid, Spain, or email eugpsr@cambridge.org

The History of Contingency and Future-Oriented Thought

Elements in Historical Theory and Practice

DOI: 10.1017/9781009358767
First published online: February 2026

Thomas Moynihan
Cambridge University

Author for correspondence: Thomas Moynihan, thomas.moynihan@gmail.com

Abstract: The future is contingent. It can unfold differently, hinging on chance or choice within the present. This Element tells the story of how these twin concepts have developed across human history. Arcing from our earliest ancestors, through al-Ghazālī, to S. J. Gould, the Element demonstrates how humans realised the future is an undecided, contingent place – at scales leading beyond the biographical, up to the planetary, and beyond. It pinpoints this realisation as an ongoing and unfinished intellectual revolution. Just as the telescope revealed Deep Space in the 1600s, and the geologists' hammer revealed Deep Time in the 1800s, contemporary developments in science are revealing what I call Deep Possibility. This is the realisation that there is far more possible than will ever be actual. It is this that makes history matter, and gives contingency its bite, insofar as it forces acknowledgement that not all outcomes will come to pass regardless.

This Element also has a video abstract:
www.cambridge.org/EHTP_Moynihan_abstract

Keywords: Future, Risk, Contingency, Extinction, Possibility

© Thomas Moynihan 2026

ISBNs: 9781009571616 (HB), 9781009358781 (PB), 9781009358767 (OC)
ISSNs: 2634-8616 (online), 2634-8608 (print)

Contents

Introduction: The Death of Destiny — 1

1 Contingency's Gestation — 9

2 Future's Dawn — 28

3 Contingency Unbound — 40

4 Conclusion: Deep Possibility in the Non-Ergodic Universe — 52

Glossary — 57

Bibliography — 60

Introduction: The Death of Destiny

The future is of interest to everyone. This is because we are all headed there, whether we like it or not. So, too, is the concept of contingency of interest to everyone. We all apply it every day, every time we commit to a decision.

For example, I understand that, if I hadn't stopped to buy a coffee, I would not have missed my bus. This is an application of the concept of contingency: of the understanding that things don't have to play out the way they in fact do, that events can go otherwise hinging on chance or choice.

This notion underwrites – at the most fundamental level – our understanding of what it even is to be an agent. Without it, the idea of freedom and responsibility makes no sense. We impute culpability when we acknowledge that the culprit *could have* acted otherwise, and, if they had done so, their crime – and the consequent harm – would not have been committed.

These twin concepts, of contingency and futurity, are amongst the most important concepts we have. Historically speaking, their combined application has been responsible for the sparking of every single progressive movement, reformation, or renovation. It is only by understanding that the way of the world is not inevitable, and can thus be otherwise, that anyone has ever intentionally attempted to make it otherwise. Understanding this sits beneath all of history's attempts to make the future a better, more just, place; it foments all attempts to overcome the errors and prejudices of the past.

This way, the concepts of contingency and futurity are also inextricably linked. In our personal lives, we care about our future because our decisions and actions *influence* that future. And actions only matter, or exert influence, if the consequences they unleash would not otherwise have happened. That is, if they are *contingent*. Their influence rests in the recognition that, had they not taken place, then everything afterward would have unfolded differently too. Moreover, they matter more in proportion to how *lasting* these impacts are – and peerlessly so if they cannot be reversed. Or, in other words are *indelible*.

Sometimes, applying these concepts is matter of life or death. I understand that if I injure myself severely enough, I may die prematurely, which is an outcome which cannot be reversed. Because I know such an outcome is not inevitable, I daily endeavour to avoid it.

We are very fluent with these concepts – of indelibility and contingency as applied to the future – when it comes to our own biographies. But, as we enter the so-called Anthropocene, our wider societies are increasingly struggling with the fact that they now undeniably must be applied much further beyond, to the biography of the planet itself.

That is, our societies now daily struggle with the fact that what happens now has the potential to alter the future for Earth's entire biosphere. In forms of nuclear waste, climate disruption, resource extraction, and mass extinction, we now recognise the arena – wherein what comes before can influence everything coming after, in ways that aren't inevitable – has expanded far beyond the traditional remit of human affairs: having spilt into the deeper past, and further future, of Earth's unfolding biosphere. Humankind now has the power to indelibly scar the planet's future. The concepts of 'contingency' and 'consequence' have, by awful necessity, been stretched to the scale of globe and giga-annum.

These are the stakes, providing a backdrop against which all our private aspirations and anxieties must unfold. Putting such stakes into further relief, science now has a firm sense of how much past is behind, and how much future could be left ahead, for life on Earth.

We now understand the universe itself is roughly 14 billion years old and the Earth around 4 billion years old. Though life appears to have begun shortly thereafter, complex life – with skeletons for mobility and nervous systems to sense – has been around for something like half a billion years. *Homo sapiens*, by contrast, has only existed for something like three hundred thousand years. Recorded history, following the invention of writing, is even shorter, spanning only around five millennia so far. The radiometric dating techniques that produced all these estimates have only been around for a century or so.

By contrast, experts today predict that the future for complex life on Earth is something on the order of one to one and a half billion years.[1] On this view, compared to the past required to produce us, our species has *only just* appeared; but, already, the deleterious effects of our activities are being projected over a potentially protracted future.

Entering the third millennium, it is not just facts *about* human existence, or the wider biosphere, that are acknowledged to be contingent: the fact *of* human existence, and a thriving biosphere, has also become contingent.[2]

There *could* be a lengthy, vibrant future for biology on Earth. Or, in the absolute worst case, no future at all. The aeons-long evolutionary epic that produced us, alongside all our fellow species, *could* produce more diversity and grandeur. Or it could end within a lifetime.

We must now acknowledge that the events in the present, going one way rather than any other, may alter the planet's entire future: permanently filtering all that comes after, in irreversible, yet entirely contingent, ways.

---

[1] Wolf & Toon, 'Evolution of Habitable Climates'. [2] Ord, *The Precipice*.

What follows is the story of how we got here. Even being aware of our predicament is a vast intellectual achievement, millennia and generations in the making. As with all concepts, our modern notions of contingency and futurity did not emerge from nowhere nor did they arrive fully formed. Concepts, like creatures, evolve: in that they are products of cumulated intricacy, and never arrive *sui generis*. Their evolution takes trial and error, and cumulation and constellation of evidence, which, in turn, takes time.[3]

Though humans now comfortably apply the concept of contingency beyond their own lives, onto a future stretching far beyond, this has not always been so. The reason is simple. For most of history, the evidence to prove such concepts apply beyond our own lives was lacking. It remained *underdetermined* as to whether nature, at scales larger than our own personal biographical bookends, exhibits contingency and irreversibility. There wasn't yet the evidence to decide, conclusively and collectively, either way: it hadn't yet been uncovered.

This underdetermination applied *everywhere* on the globe prior to its circumnavigation, for obvious reasons. Nonetheless, it should be noted that – despite spanning Europe and the Middle East – the following focuses on how this underdetermination was undone within the Western, scientific tradition. Other notions of contingency and futurity exist in other traditions: from the Indigenous Kulin tribes of South-Eastern Australia, who believed their universe would end if they didn't maintain their axe exchanges; to Ancient Egyptian claims it is "good to speak to posterity"; to the traditional Chinese belief in "*Tian*", as a cosmic principle maintaining moral order in the world, over and above human agency and volition. Richly divergent, historical developments of notions in these traditions will have taken very different lines to those recounted below, but given confines of the Element a truly global treatment cannot be explored here.

The following, then, is the story of how the modern scientific worldview's notion of contingency was pieced together, thus ballooning not only our sense of

---

[3] Of course, in practice, inquiry is messy and uneven: Undergirded by a patchwork of competing worldviews, impelled by divergent motivations. Few of the writers, philosophers, and scientists discussed in this Element would have acknowledged they were working in a unified tradition, contributing to the building up of a single idea. Yet science produces consilience as much as it involves revolutions and ruptures. The following, then, is an attempt at 'recollective rationality' or 'recollective reconstruction', to borrow terms from philosopher Robert Brandom: That is, to bring a continuity to past inquiry which, at the time, could not have been prospected by the inquirers themselves. Medieval theologians had no idea *that* their conceptual innovations would contribute to the modern scientific method's birth, and yet contribute they nonetheless did. Some accounts may highlight what's incommensurable, this foregrounds what's cumulative, even if accidentally so. The history of thought, like the history of the world, is contingent – yet contingency doesn't preclude continuity. See Brandom, *A Spirit of Trust*.

how much time might be ahead, but also our estimation of how divergently it might permanently play out.

Indeed, properly grappling with the future is never just about gauging how much further time could be ahead. It also involves uncovering how divergently everything about the present would be if events in the past, which didn't need to have happened, had played out differently. Because, only by coming to terms with this, do we grapple with just how *open* and *contingent* what's ahead might also be.

Let's call this the Horizon of Contingency, though it could just as well be called the Horizon of Consequence. This describes that arena of space and time wherein people acknowledge *history matters* because what can happen in the future is not independent of what's happened in the past. That is, that arena where what comes after is recognised as *contingent upon* what came before, in the sense that, had previous events gone otherwise, then everything afterward would have played out differently also.

This arena – this horizon – extends, from the present moment, outward into both the past and the future: making up the tapestry of influences, without which the present wouldn't be what it is; alongside the cascade of downstream impacts, dictating the direction in which all future moments flow.

It also extends outward, from the human perspective, into space. Because knowledge is tethered to observation, we only *know* so far as we – or our tools – can *see*. This way, before humans invented clever ways to survey scales greater than the immediate, it was impossible to disqualify hunches that – beyond the purview of what's humanly tangible – time exhibits reversibility and all possibilities eternally recur.

This is why this shared horizon, though it is set by knowledge's shifting frontiers, is materially important. It informs behaviour. How far people have acknowledged it to stretch – beyond our individual biographies – has itself changed over time, as our species has increasingly gained our bearings *within* time.

So, what lies beyond the acknowledged Horizon of Contingency, at least in the estimation of those doing the acknowledging? Here, things aren't necessarily assumed timeless or static. Things here can and do change – grow and decay – but just not in a way that is thought to have *persisting direction in time*.

On one level, this is to do with estimation of the range of contingency, or the scope of unrealised possibility. Counterintuitively, history is interesting – and exerts its influence on the future – *because of all the things that didn't actually happen*. It is the entrenching of certain prior possibilities, to the exclusion of others, that explains why the present is the way it is rather than any other way. It is *this* that makes decisions or events consequential. They only matter when not every possible outcome will eventually come to pass regardless.

But, for most of human history, it could be legitimately assumed that the space of historic possibility was small enough, and the time or space available comparatively large enough, that – beyond the known Horizon of Contingency – all possibilities would exhaustively manifest and thereafter recur and repeat. At the very least, until recently, there wasn't yet the evidence to satisfactorily disqualify such assumption, beyond scales much more encompassing than the singular human lifespan.

Another way to flesh this out is by borrowing two concepts from physics. There are two types of systems, ergodic ones and non-ergodic ones. An example of an ergodic system is one which reliably visits and revisits *all* its possible states with a null likelihood of *never* returning to any one of them. Given enough time, its past and future will eventually look indistinguishable. In technical parlance, it is *memoryless*.

Contrarily, an example of a non-ergodic system is one which will not pass through all its possible states, because the manifestation of certain possibilities in the past – to the permanent exclusion of others – irreversibly constrains everything that can possibly happen thereafter. Such systems exhibit *absorbing states*: regions of the system's possibility space which, upon entry, can never be exited. Accordingly, once it has entered such a region, the system's entire future will end up looking fundamentally and irreversibly different from its extended past – *no matter how much time is available*. This way, such systems exhibit *irreversibility* and *memory*. Applied to evolution, extinction is a brilliant example of an absorbing state for a species.

The ergodic and non-ergodic distinction is crucial, again, because history only enters the picture – and is able to contingently and irreversibly influence the future – when not everything that can happen does eventually happen. Beyond the horizon of the measured and recorded, it has long been assumed that the spans of space and time are effectively boundless, such that nature's *entire* space of possibility is exhaustively manifested and limitlessly remanifested. After all, given enough rolls of a many-sided dice – either sequentially or simultaneously – all possibilities will be made manifest and reliably repeat.

What's at stake throughout the following is the question of whether nature, beyond familiar and tangible scales, exhibits history, irreversibility, memory, and non-ergodicity in this sense, such that events in the expanded and extended past can indelibly and contingently influence the expanded and extended future. Answers to this question, as we will soon see, have drastically changed over the centuries.

This matters practically because, beyond the acknowledged Horizon of Contingence, all influence of the past and present on the future therefore eventually washes away: the legacy of things going on track, rather than any other, will eventually become irrelevant, because the alternate paths and possibilities remain accessible and will, given enough time, inevitably recur limitlessly.

Over the longer run, there is thus no direction, no persistence, no memory. All impacts, eventually, are reversed, washing out into their opposites. All losses are eventually recouped and compensated, as what is lost is returned. Beyond the established Horizon of Contingency, it is possible to believe that all processes are memoryless and meandering, thus neutering any acknowledged impact of what happens here and now at this larger, non-local scale.

This is of crucial consideration. Within the Horizon, the course of past events matters practically; beyond it, the course of past events is absolved of mattering, at least permanently or persistently. Everything returns in eternity and infinity. It is only in bounded time, time with known dimensions or extremities, that death or loss can be forever.

So, whilst you can feel avoidable losses or local damages keenly within what you acknowledge as the Horizon of Contingency, you can always point beyond it – to that larger scale or interval wherein you assume what's lost must be returned – in order to remedy or diminish the sense of immediate damage.

For the longest time, this is precisely what people have done – when it comes to scales of space and time beyond the observable – in order to assuage themselves of fear that accidents and losses *really* matter. For example, people used to palliate the potential for humanity's extinction on Earth by claiming that our species must inevitably return throughout the cosmic vastitudes of time and space.

Indeed, the Horizon of Contingency is the arena within which concepts like 'loss', 'extinction', and 'squander' gain their full bite: because, beyond it, they are defanged by cycling returns, wherein everything lost is later regained.

Indeed, as we shall see, following the Copernican revolution, from roughly the 1600s up until sometime in the earlier 1900s, many people presumed everything happening on Earth was bound to repeat elsewhere, such that what happened next for our planet *didn't really matter*. They pronounced that we cannot be the first, nor last, exemplar of humankind in this universe. At least, such a proposal had *not yet been* satisfactorily disconfirmed. But science, as will later be explored, has lately demonstrated it almost certainly false.

It did so by putting bookends on cosmic time. What follows is the story of how gauging the placement of the present within this unfolding volume – at increasingly encompassing scales – proves what happens next might just be of significance, not only locally, but far further afield.

Demonstrating this took millennia of inquiry. It took confirming that, in this universe, there was a beginning and will be an end to *all things*. Only by determining this has modern science thrown into crisp relief the truth that what we do *might* resonate everlastingly. Because, if time has extremities, then history will never repeat; and if what's happening here and now will never reoccur, certain decisions can never be taken back or reversed.

On another level, this has also all flowed from increasing appreciation that what's unrealised far outstrips what's been realised. Again, historically, given available evidence, it was legitimate to assume that nature's range of possibilities is comparatively small, and the time or space available comparatively large, such that all potentials will necessarily have already played out, somewhere or somewhen, and will be returned to. This, of course, removes indelibility and contingency from the picture, beyond local scales. Again, history only matters – and alters its future – when not everything that *can* happen *does* happen. It is this that makes contingency resonate, as not all outcomes will play out regardless.

Of course, this historic assumption makes perfect sense. Millennia ago, there wasn't a global archaeological and fossil record collated, such that it was impossible to falsify suspicion that human possibilities haven't simply been exhaustively cycling since time immemorial. Or, that everything happening right now has already happened before and will recur again on unknown landmasses. And this, as we shall soon see, is precisely what premodern people largely assumed. Later, when such a view began becoming untenable during the Renaissance, the size of the universe radically expanded thanks to telescopes, such that it became plausible to now suppose everything happening here and now had already happened – or was concurrently unfolding – on other planets in the infinity of space.

Darwin's great insight was that, of all the organisms terrestrially possible, only a select few have and will exist. It is this that allowed him to *explain* why life looks the way it does today rather than any other way: because certain animals reproduced in the past, to the permanent exclusion of other possible lineages. Nonetheless, of course, the role of chance and contingency in the *origin of life* itself seemingly remained obscured until the mid-1900s. Up until then, people assumed it would pop up wherever possible in the cosmos. What's more, it took a while for the scope of contingency in its basic building blocks – that is, the latitude for other plausible architectures – to also bed in.

Which is all to say, the tenor and tone of much scientific advance over the centuries can be seen as a further throwing into relief of the fact that *there's far more possible than is actual*, or, *there's far more unrealised than is realised*. And, of course, the degree to which we have accepted this is also the degree to which we've realised that Earth's life is cosmically unique (and, thus, cosmically endangered). There may be life elsewhere, but will be unimaginably different. This is a shockingly modern insight. It is why we should care the future of life on Earth, because it won't be repeating anywhere, ever again. The future is in our hands. There won't be retries.

This way, the degree to which accumulating insight has expanded the Horizon of Contingency, from our own bookended biographies outward into the cosmos, is the extent to which the stakes – of what unfolds next, here and now – have heightened. It is this knowledge – about the wider universe and its workings – which, as we shall see, has brought home the truth to us that extinction is truly forever.

This way, increasing sensitivity to contingency is a unifying theme of modern science, often providing the leading edge of inquiry's expanding shockfront against the unknown and uncertain. As the telescope dethroned our sense of space in the 1500s and 1600s, and the geologist's hammer decentred us in time in the 1700s and 1800s, much of modern knowledge is revealing everything locally actual to be a tiny island within a much wider space of what's unrealised. This gives contingency bite. We talk of the discovery of Deep Time, and of Deep Space; the following is the story of how we discovered what I call Deep Possibility.

Deep Possibility is the recognition that *there's far more that is possible than is actual*. Science's expansion of the acknowledged space of the possible over the actual is heavily tied, in recent times, to the development of the electronic computer and the birth of computer-dependent fields like chaos theory. Like the telescope before it, the introduction of the computer – and of simulation – in the 1900s made new vistas visible. Because simulation makes tangible that what *actually happens* is often a tiny subset within the much wider space of *what can*. Accordingly, just as humankind's sense of 'here' and 'now' has been decentred within progressively vaster volumes of space and time, so too is everything 'actual' being revealed to be a tiny archipelago within an increasingly vast ocean of possibilities unrealised.

Though this contemporary sense of Deep Possibility is clearly resultant upon science's increasingly sophisticated capacities for simulation, it can be nonetheless seen as the culmination of a much longer process of inquiry: a process wherein inquirers – across the generations – have had to come to terms with contingency at increasingly encompassing scales of time and of space. What follows is an account of how that unfolded.

1 Contingency's Gestation

1.1 Palaeolithic: The first counterfactual

In 1939, J.R.R. Tolkien defined what he called a 'eucatastrophe', articulating it as an unexpected yet joyous turn: 'a sudden and miraculous grace'. Like a catastrophe, being an unprecedented break from the prior course of events – *but for the better*.[4]

Eighteen years later, the Harvard astronomer Harlow Shapley similarly spoke of the 'Great Moments' of history, defining them similarly. His candidates included the Big Bang – which led to the formation of the matter we are made from – alongside the evolution of photosynthesis on Earth and the accumulated accidents allowing the first animals to leave the ocean for the land.[5]

Here's another candidate for a eucatastrophe, or, a great turning in the course of the world. Somewhere within Africa, probably tens of thousands of years ago, potentially hundreds of thousands, a string of sounds fell from the lips of one of our forebears. It expressed, for the first time, what properly could be called a counterfactual.

It might have been expressed in awe, in urgency, in annoyance. We will never know. The utterer will forever remain nameless and unsung. But it was the first linguistic utterance, articulated on this planet, describing something not currently actual. Instead, it was about something else: *the way world could be or could become*. It was the entrance of the future into our linguistic world. It was the birth of all our tomorrows.

Counterfactuals are part of modal discourse. Modal discourse is the family of locutions expressing states of affairs that are not currently actual, or, in other words are *irrealis*. They empower a language to express modalities: phrases tracking which things are possible or impossible, contingent or necessary, permissible or impermissible, and conditional one upon another.

Of course, anticipation exists across life's tree, with evidence of prevision stretching from horse to hymenopteran. In one sense, a nervous system *just is* a machine for predicting one's environment. Forms of foresight clearly have evolved piecemeal and multiply across life's tree. But humans are uniquely empowered when it comes to predicting the future.

Psychologists talk about 'mental time travel': the ability to recall the past and predict the future.[6] This affords us capacity not only to *keep track* of our biographies, but, also, to a degree, to *actively author them*. It allows us to

---

[4] Tolkien, 'On Fairy-Stories'.
[5] Shapley, 'Digression on Great Moments'. More recently, the proponent of 'big history' David Christian referred to similar developments as 'threshold events'.
[6] Suddendorf et al., *Invention of Tomorrow*.

learn from yesterday, so as to pursue preferable tomorrows. Our unique aptitude at 'mental time travel' rests, almost certainly, on human language and its unique capacity to talk about a world that is otherwise than the one currently, immediately perceived.[7]

Inventing the whole suite of linguistic aptitudes required for this would not have been one clean event. Nonetheless, though anatomically modern humans have existed for something like 300,000 years, behaviourally modern humans emerged around 70,000 years ago. The former *looked* like us; the latter *acted* like us. They planned, danced, created symbols, told stories, and began accumulating traditions. Nobody today knows exactly why this happened, but it's easy to imagine it was caused by – or itself helped cause – an expansion in what our language was capable of expressing.

Perhaps hominids had long been accumulating rich vocabularies of declaration and denotation: anchored purely in the here and now, picking out immediately present objects or events. Perhaps innovations were thereafter made, enabling the embedding of such denotive exclamations within modal constructions. Any shared, complex language presumably needs such constructions, because they allow rules – and, thus, what's correct and incorrect, or grammatical and ungrammatical – to be articulated and maintained. Rules express what ought to be: in excess of what's actual, irrespective of whether they are always followed; and no amount of declarations of fact can capture this unique, motivating aspect to their meaning.

Such *irrealis* constructions, moreover, would have initiated our species into a world of right and wrong – or, at least, where these are recognisable concepts, in addition to guttural feelings, because they are now explicable. The difference between what 'ought' and 'is' rests, after all, in the fact that former doesn't need to exist to be meaningful. Norms will have existed long before creatures could talk about them – in some diffuse way, as appetites or conventions – but now they could be discussed, contested, disputed, discarded. Pragmatically, this would have impressively empowered those vocabularies of diplomacy necessary for better cooperation: for resolution of dispute and division of labour.

What's more, being able to talk about what isn't (yet) real is likely attached to 'mental synthesis': the capacity for stitching together images in one's imagination, into a combination not previously perceived. Combining a wooden stick with a knapped stone, for example, plucks a hatchet from inexistence.[8]

Investing in better tools and cooperating more fluidly mean more surplus time and energy. This diminishes current pressures on survival, opening room for

---

[7] Suddendorf et al., 'Mental Time Travel'.
[8] Vyshedskiy, 'Language Evolution to Revolution'.

luxuries such as planning more and further ahead, freeing up more resources for further invention. It's a loop. *Thinking about the future caused more thinking about the future.*

By the point this delaminates imaginative horizons from a single lifetime, this would also galvanise the precept of passing recipes and techniques forward – via teaching and tutelage. A stock of insight starts building *across* generations, rather than resetting with the passing of each one, meaning wisdom instead becomes an intergenerationally building stock. Anthropologists call this 'cumulative culture'.[9]

By being able to talk about how things ought to be – in excess of how they merely are – human beings could come not only to declare things about the world but also to assess the accuracy of such declarations. A totalitarianism of sensation became accountability to a reality. Indeed, if an utterance or internal state cannot even be said to be wrong, how can it purport to have a world in view: to describe it by being held accountable to it?

Whenever and wherever all this came fell into place, our species dislocated itself from the barricades of the cloistered present – from the absolutism of the actual – in a fashion more intense than any species before. Our kind stepped forth into the spacious world of what's merely possible: of what-could-have-been; of what-could-yet-be.

The cumulation of the first modal utterances embarked our species on an adventure. Though they couldn't have foreseen it, the heirloom they bequeathed hoisted *Homo sapiens* out of the pressing present, eventually coaxing the human mind not only into the deepest past and furthest future but also towards reverse engineering the very workings of the world. And knowing how to imagine the world otherwise is the first step towards making it otherwise. The future is made from motivation as much as prediction.

Our ancestors, when they first started talking this way, began drifting from somewhere and somewhen towards less parochial vantages, and we have been drifting ever since – becoming disoriented and dislocated from the concrete present, but freer in the process. The Horizon of Contingency could begin to expand beyond the fleeting present, forcing unfolding encounters with the truth that the world is chancy and its future is undecided, in ways applying outside the confines of a single, fleeting life.

At the limit, being able to discuss the contingent truth of our claims ultimately opened out into acknowledgement of the contingency of truth-seeking and claim-making itself: eventually flowing into modern awareness that nothing about the human mind is a necessary feature of independent nature. Or, in other

---

[9] Vale et al., 'Cumulative Culture and Future Thinking'.

words, awareness our species – and everything it cares about – can go extinct, never to return.

Whether all this proves a 'eucatastrophe' or a 'catastrophe' is yet to be decided. The decision, in the main, is down to us and those coming next.

1.2 Ancient: That the World Is All It Can Be

Piercing the absolutism of immediacy, seeing a world of expanded possibility beyond, modal speak bequeathed to our ancestors a way of negotiating the world that wasn't governed by the exigencies of sensation nor tethered to the overwhelming present. It cleaved open the room to step back from what is, in order to assess what could – and should – be.

This explains why humans developed agriculture, eventually encouraging urban centres to tumesce, sometime around 10,000 years ago. These advances can be seen as amongst the first widescale, albeit *ad hoc*, attempts at mitigating and distributing risk – oriented, by definition, at protecting tomorrow's interests.

Efforts to predict, and thus control, the future remained limited to related techniques for the majority of recorded history. That is, as extemporaneous buffers against unpredictable nature: dams and dikes to protect against flooding; stockpiling and crop rotations to prevent famine; city walls and guards to defend against invasions. This, for the longest time, was the cutting-edge technology for manipulating the future.

During the Twelfth Dynasty of Egypt's Middle Kingdom, Amenemhat III dammed the entire Nile. After fires in Rome in AD 6, Emperor Augustus set up a citywide force of firefighters. These evidence anticipation of risks and coordinated attempts to mitigate them. But these were all *post hoc* preparations for familiar catastrophes: calamities already within the record; disasters that were known to have happened. They evince responsivity to the precedented, not yet the unprecedented.

This connects to a truth summarised by the American historian Robert Heilbroner. He reflected, of the 'first stratified societies', that 'dynastic dreams were dreamt and visions of triumph or ruin entertained':

> but there is no mention in the papyri and cuneiform tablets on which these hopes and fears were recorded that they envisaged, in the slightest degree, changes in the material conditions of the great masses, or for that matter, of the ruling class itself.[10]

This observation appears to be true. It seems odd to us now: but the idea humanity's future could be not only radically different but also different in unpredictable ways is a shockingly recent addition to worldviews.

---

[10] Heilbroner, *Visions of the Future*, p.8.

One plausible explanation for this is simple. There just wasn't yet enough recorded history for anyone to *notice* such change *can* happen. It is, after all, the historic record that provides determinate proof that human values and views transform over time. But, without a sufficient evidential chronicle available, it wouldn't be clear this happens.

Sometimes called the oldest book in the world, the Ancient Egyptian *Instructions of Ptahhotep*, composed 4000 years ago, makes it clear that it 'is good to speak to posterity'.[11]

Ancient Egyptians argued the best accomplishments are those that become lasting monuments. With their towering pyramids, they evidently aimed to leave a lasting impression. This implies concern for an extended future. However, it is unclear whether they fretted much about whether distant future generations – that is, us – would *look upon* these monuments the same way *they* looked upon them. It's unlikely the architects of the pyramids considered posterity might come to scrutinise and study their works – to interpret or misinterpret them – through the unfamiliar eyes of an unrecognisably alien epoch. There's scant evidence they suffered any *anxiety of interpretation*: angst about their beliefs *not* standing the test of time. Such monuments, indeed, can be read as evidence of precisely the opposite.

Point being, in the long millennia since, humanity's collective memory has expanded. With the cumulative increase in chronicling and compiling of records, people have progressively come to appreciate the past really *is* a foreign country. It's very simple. As recorded time has gone on, there's been more evidence for the truth of this: and building recognition that things *have been* different dovetails into building anticipation that they *may become* different again. (Which nurtures awareness – and anxiety – that the future might look back on your present with very different eyes.)

Relatedly, before a global archaeological and fossil record was compiled, cross-referenced, and communicated across continents – rather than remaining constrained within one – it wasn't possible to *falsify* hunches that human history has been cycling on Earth, without definitively beginning, throughout boundless ages.

As we shall later see, such a planetwide record would only begin being pieced together much later: throughout the 1700s and 1800s. Accordingly, for most of human history, people were liable to assume that human history has been going, much in the same way, forever, and would so continue. That everything they were witnessing on their landmass had already been chronicled or achieved

---

[11] Lichtheim, *Ancient Egyptian Literature*, vol.I, p.73.

elsewhere, on uncontacted continents, or in forgotten aeons. Again, there was not yet evidence to disqualify such assumption.

Accordingly, the Ancient Greeks and Romans, for example, tended to assume that time was eternal and that the future would thus, in the longer term, look like the past. It was invariably assumed that humanity's combined possibilities – the total space of human potential – were small enough, and the time or space available comparatively large enough, that this entire set of possibilities would exhaustively manifest and thereafter recur and repeat without limit.

This is why Thucydides, writing around 400 BC, thought that chronicling his local history was indefinitely instructive for the future: precisely because possibilities are 'repeated', such that 'human nature' never truly changes.[12]

But another explanation for Heilbroner's observation rests in language itself. After all, accumulating insight about the world comes not only from accumulated encounters with it but from clarifications in the ways *we talk about it*. Refinements in our awareness of what it is our languages are *doing* when we describe the world, and what they aren't doing, allow our languages to better model that world. And, as with all other forms of discovery, this takes time.

Thucydides's sentiment can be tied, that is, to a conception of possibility prevalent throughout the premodern world, which defined it as *'that which sometimes happens'*. This was by contrast to necessity, defined as *'that which always happens'*, and impossibility, as *'that which never happens'*.

This has been called the 'statistical interpretation of modality'. It tethers modal definitions to 'temporal frequency', or, concrete realisation in time.[13] Put differently, it's the same as saying 'nothing that's possible never happens'. Though this basic assumption pre-existed him, it was first made explicit by Aristotle, who was the first to attempt to clarify what we actually mean when we deploy modal language.[14] In the *Metaphysics*, for example, Aristotle evidenced his assumption by declaring that 'evidently it cannot be true to say *'this is capable of being but will not be'*'.[15] This formulation thus limits possibility to what is called a 'diachronic' conception: tethering it to what actually happens in time, thus blunting conception of entirely unrealised possibilities. Across his corpus, Aristotle consistently defines 'impossible' as what is never the case; 'necessary', as what is always the case; and 'possible', as what is sometimes the case.[16]

---

[12] Thucydides, *Peloponesian War*, p.48. [13] Hintikka, *Time and Necessity*.
[14] Borghini, *Metaphysics of Modality*, p.27.
[15] Aristotle, *Metaphysics*, 1047b8-9. All references to Aristotle are from *The Complete Works*, translated by Jonathon Barnes.
[16] Hintikka, *Time and Necessity*.

Though elegantly intuitive, this formulation obstructs articulation of possibilities that have never once happened before.[17] It blunts sensitivity, in other words, to entirely unprecedented potentials. Writing in *De Caelo*, Aristotle revealingly reasoned that nothing which has *always* existed can be 'destructible', because the possibility of its destruction would, necessarily, *have already come to pass*.[18] Combined with his belief in the eternity of the past, this becomes the uninspected assumption that there is no such thing as a genuine unprecedented possibility.

Aristotle – and other premodern thinkers – readily applied this to wider nature as much as to human history, assuming things simply cycle limitlessly, and everything that can happen already has happened.[19] Hence, they lacked the idea that the further future – at the largest and most systemic scales – could come to look drastically different from the extended past. This, understandably, would have gelled comfortably with their lived experience: wherein material conditions didn't visibly alter – in undeniably novel ways – during a single lifetime.

Given assumption of a limitless past, Aristotle therefore concluded 'each art and science has often been developed as far as possible and has again perished', such that the 'same opinions appear in cycles among men'. He held this had happened 'not once nor twice nor occasionally but infinitely often'.[20] Within 'the multitude of years', he insisted, 'everything has been found out'.[21] Aristotle even elsewhere claimed the aim of inquiry is merely to rectify 'defects' in knowledge – that is, the recollection of what's forgotten.[22] Tellingly, the Greek word 'encyclopaedia' contains the word 'cylcos', implying knowledge is a returning circle.

Assuming time is 'vast and immeasurable', Plato also claimed the past is of 'an infinitely long period of time': such that, in his eyes, countless civilisations have 'come into existence', and just 'as many' have 'perished'. From this, he reasoned, their social and political arrangements have been *of every possible*

---

[17] In the most extreme form, we find this in the philosophy of Parmenides: who, living around 500 BC, reasoned from the claim 'non-being is not' that 'only being is', such that everything is necessarily all that it can be and existence strictly cannot become otherwise than it is. Plato was less extreme, noticing that when say something 'is not', we are not contradicting ourselves by saying something existent is inexistent (i.e. 'X is not'), because we are instead differing one thing from other existent things (i.e. 'X is not Y'). This way, he accommodated for things becoming other things, as a form of differentiation internal to existence, but it still led him to the view that all possibilities reliably become manifest (or, come true at some point within the timeline of our world). This, of course, still precludes the possibility of eternally unrealised potentials: which is what gives history – and its influence over the future – its bite, insofar as decisions are only consequential when not all possible outcomes come to pass regardless.
[18] Aristotle, *De Caelo*, 281b 19–25. [19] Aristotle, *Meteorology*, 352a17-25; 352b17-19.
[20] Aristotle, *Metaphysics*, 1074b10-11; *Meteorology,* 339b27-28.
[21] Aristotle, *Politics,* 1264a3. [22] Aristotle, *Politics*, 1329b25-35.

kind. Every permutation of human 'goodness' and 'badness', he assumed, must have *already* been passed through innumerably many times.[23]

By the same token, he believed all possibilities would, inevitably, be manifested again, unceasingly throughout the measureless future, regardless of what happens now. Assuming this meant assuming that no human potentials can ever be permanently lost, or irreversibly disappear from existence, including the potential for human existence as such. Indeed, Plato spoke of the

> ... periodic destruction at long intervals of the surface of the earth by massive conflagrations ...

But he also clarified that 'the human race has often been destroyed in various ways – as it will be in the future too'.[24] The supposition therefore being that, even if humankind should be entirely extinguished, it would simply endlessly return. Other thinkers, like Xenophanes, had already made similar claims.[25]

This is why the premodern world lacked our modern concept of extinction: which, by definition, involves irreversibility. There simply wasn't yet the collated evidence to determine that once species are wiped out to the final member, they are gone forever. In absence of contrary proof – which, again, wouldn't arrive until a global picture of the fossil record was pieced together – it was, again, impossible to banish presumption that eradicated species would simply, eventually, always return. Given ancient definitions of modality, after all, all possibilities – including species themselves – sometimes are not and sometimes are.[26]

More precisely, on this view, no genuine influences from the present persist into the further future, because the future will be a repeat of the past regardless of what happens now. Nothing can be lost, nothing gained. It was for this reason that, around 50 BC, Cicero claimed there was little point in seeking to impart legacies that are '*diuturnam*', or durable, much less ones that are indelible.[27]

Indeed, Cicero and many others, following Plato's initial conjectures, believed that catastrophes regularly destroyed civilisation – wiping away all accumulated learning – such that human history could all play out again, in unending cycle. This is why Lucretius entertained the possibility that everything he was witnessing in his own life – all unfolding achievements – were 'things'

---

[23] Plato, *Laws*, 676a-b; 682a-b.   [24] Plato, *Timaeus and Critias*, p.9–10.
[25] Hippolytus, *Refutation*, p.49.
[26] This is likely one reason why Lucretius proclaimed that 'time has no independent existence' apart from the events that actually happen within it. Time wasn't considered as a universal medium within which some possibilities are expressed and others are not; instead, it was often thought of as a local epiphenomenon, weaving together parochial events and what actually happens, but entirely dependent upon them. See Lucretius, *Nature of Things*, p.15.
[27] Cicero, *De Re Publica*, p.90.

which had 'happened before': it's simply that countless earlier 'races of human beings perished in great conflagration' and their achievements 'were razed by a mighty convulsion of the world'.[28] Once more, ahead of sizeable evidence to the contrary, there wasn't yet the combined evidence to disprove such suspicion.

But what of Plato's *Republic*? Surely, he was thinking of something unprecedented when delineating his utopian vision for ideal society. Not so: midway through the dialogue, Plato has Socrates explicate he is envisioning a situation that 'has been' in the 'infinite time past' – or, otherwise, is 'now' in some 'region far beyond our ken' – such that we can also be sure it will inevitably return again 'hereafter'.[29]

For the ancient world, therefore, given limitations of compiled evidence as much as limitations of language, possibility was inherently tethered to prior manifestation, such that cogently articulating the entirely unprecedented was stymied. This is why, as Heilbroner observed, the premodern universe lacked our modern conception of the future: as undecided and undetermined and populated by what's unprecedented and unpredictable. Indeed, Aristotle readily affirmed that 'it is of actual things already existing that we acquire knowledge': which is the same as denying we concretely can know anything about things which haven't yet existed.[30] If we can't talk of things that aren't already actual, then the only way we can talk of the future is as a loop of the past.

Given available knowledge, on balance, it was – back then – safer to assume time was eternal and all possibilities simply cycle, such that the future would, in the longer term, be a repeat of the past and all present influences be laundered away. The Horizon of Contingency was, thus, limited in scope to one's own lifetime and, at most, one's own polis or nation. Beyond that, it was impossible to verify new things can happen and old things can be irreversibly lost across an undetermined, undecided future. The future remained shallow.

1.3 Medieval: That the World Could Have Been Otherwise

Similar definitions of possibility – and, thus, assumptions about the future – persisted well into the Medieval Era. Glossing Aristotle around AD 1100, the Arabic philosopher Ibn Rushd explained that 'the term 'possible' is used' to talk either of that which 'happens more often than not' or 'less often than not'.[31] Modality remained tied to diachronic definitions and to manifestation in time: subtly precluding the possibility of the entirely unprecedented; reducing contingency to variations upon what's already been.

---

[28] Lucretius, *Nature of Things*, p.146.   [29] Plato, *Republic*, 6.499c-d.
[30] Aristotle, *Categories*, 7b24-5.   [31] Averroes, *Tahāfut al-tahāfut*, pp.1–2.

This keyed into a wider feature of much premodern belief: *the assumption that the world is inherently reasonable*. For if all possibilities at some point come to pass, the only things that are never actual must be so for demonstrable reasons of logical incoherence or contradiction – rather than by dint of brute facticity or arbitrariness. This is the same as assuming that our world is maximally rational. Or, that things are the way they are for entirely demonstrable reasons – exhaustively amenable to deductive analysis – such that they couldn't justifiably have been made otherwise than they are. (Note that this is incompatible with the modern notion of a 'law of nature': as a parameter or constraint that could plausibly have been otherwise; or, is the way it is for weaker reasons than lack of logical contradiction.)[32] This, in turn, underwrote a perennial Scholastic platitude: '*ens est bonum convertuntur*', or, 'being and good are convertible terms'. As Aristotle originally had it, 'in all things, we affirm, nature always strikes for the better'.[33]

In a yet broader sense, such belief was again consequent upon narrow definitions of modal terms. Insofar as their usage was restricted to straightforward descriptions of events *within* the world, their more subtle application – as evaluations of our conceptual frame *upon that world* – remained implicit and undeployed. Put simply, if contingency narrowly refers only denotatively to things, it has not yet been critically applied to our concepts about things. Prior to the elaboration, explication, and deployment of this meta-descriptive dimension of concepts like contingency, as picking out the limitations and uncertainties of rational judgement itself, it was thus natural for thinkers to fail to catch sight of the distinction between our moral expectations and independent reality.[34]

Nonetheless, the introduction – and eventual ascendency – of Abrahamic religion had introduced an 'alien intrusion' within the pagan worldview.[35] With the spread of Christianity and, later Islam, across the European and Arabic worlds, there arrived a sense of crisp direction in time: stretched between the twin extremities of Genesis and Judgement. The Hellenistic sense of eternalism was eventually toppled by Abrahamic belief in universal chronology.

On the one hand, eternity still saturates these creeds. Worldly time was conceived of as but a brief hiatus, environed by two eternities: a vanishing

---

[32] Hintikka, 'Leibniz on Plenitude'.   [33] Aristotle, *Generation & Corruption*, I.336b1 25–30.
[34] Put differently, by limiting modal terms to narrowly fact-stating usages, all they can do is reiterate an assumed identity between our conceptual framework and factual existence. Truncating talk of possibility to that which is 'sometimes the case' results in it only ever expressing trivial alterations within one received world-picture, rather than facilitating judgements between competing world-pictures. Limited thusly, possibility shrinks into reference to trivial rearrangements *within* one 'world', rather than picking out non-trivial distinctions *across* multiple ones, such that it cannot properly articulate the possibility that the intuitive or received world-picture is fundamentally incorrect or incomplete.
[35] Milton, 'Concept of the "Laws of Nature"', p.187.

'vale of tears' cleft between the boundless precedent of an uncreated divinity and, afterward, the unending afterlife promised for the souls He created.

On the other hand, the 'intrusive' element was immense. Jesus's crucifixion on Golgotha split history in two. For his disciples, at least, it introduced a crisp *'before'* and *'after'*: absolving all humans of their sins – everywhere – thus being incapable of precedent, reversal, or repetition. Everything afterward – that is, the future – would be different.

Previously, there was no universal reference point against which to orient 'now'. Indeed, Aristotle had once reasoned that, if history cycles, we cannot properly say we come *after* our ancestors, because, in another sense, we also come *before* them.[36] For believers in the new Abrahamic creeds, such reasoning could no longer apply. God can only sacrifice himself once, after all. If one time was not enough to get the job done then the act – of universal salvation, of the saving of the souls of everyone, everywhere – wouldn't have been fulfilled. Divinity, *being omnipotent*, doesn't work in half-measures.

Which is to say, Jesus's crucifixion was, to his disciples, undeniably an event that had never once happened before. Precisely the same applied, for early Muslims, to the arrival of the Prophet Muhammad's teachings around a half-millennium later.

These beliefs would – slowly but surely – disband elder conviction that the future must also be a closed-off repeat of the extended past. But this, as yet, was far from an acceptance of historic contingency: that is, sensitisation to the fact that the past could have played out differently, thus leading up to an unrecognisable present; nor that the future can play out multiply, depending upon what happens now.

This was because, for Muslims and Christians alike, the arc of events – from Creation to Judgement – was exhaustively orchestrated, from outside worldly time, by divine diktat. In its broadest brushstrokes, history's unfolding was considered predetermined, which, again, was highly compatible with a solely 'diachronic' conception of possibility. The things that can happen exhaust the things that will happen: hence, determinism.

Apocalypse was thus conceived of as the ultimate – unavoidable – culmination of God's infallible judgement, inscrutable though this may remain for mortals. It is important here to note that apocalyptic prophecy is distinct from the modern art of prediction, though they both are oriented towards the future, in that only the latter embeds awareness of its own corrigibility. The former does not – indeed, this is its very appeal – such that it cannot be sensitive to possibilities beyond its ken, or, indeed, assent.

---

[36] Aristotle, *Problemata*, 916a18-38.

This, again, appealed to the wider belief that ours is a maximally rational universe: where everything is the way it is – and not otherwise – for revealable reasons. Such conviction was inherited from Aristotelianism and sustained into Christian Scholasticism and Islamic Kalām. As Anselm of Canterbury proclaimed around 1080 AD: *'whatever is, is right'*.[37]

But it also played into to a view that, though worldly things could change, they couldn't do so in meaningful nor multifarious ways. In the words of Nicholas of Autrecourt, 'nothing in the universe, either in particular or in general, can be useless, for, if it were, then it would be better for it not to be than to be'.[38] Such conviction, again, prohibits irreversible loss. Because, if any existent thing ceases to be permanently, it leaves a gratuitous gap in creation, where something could be, but simply *never is again*. This was simply incompatible with underlying conviction the universe itself is maximally just, as it would introduce an unjustifiable chasm in creation's fabric. By the same token, a genuine novelty would reveal what was previously an imperfection – a vacuity of value, an empty vessel.

The uninspected assumption was that what seems morally unjustifiable must be naturally impossible. Thus, having declared that 'we feel displeasure when we believe that a thing has become non-existent', Nicolas of Autrecourt further reasoned that the universe must, across time, contain an equal amount of its possibilities, insofar as it needs to be 'always perfect to the same extent'. It must, over time, house an invariant 'complement of good'.[39] Variation in overarching 'good', after all, would introduce imperfection into creation. In other words, the aggregate 'goodness' in the universe is not contingent, is not a variable that can alter *contingent upon* local events or happenstances. If something bad happens here, something good happens over there, balancing out the whole. Again, this ties into definitions of possibility as that which sometimes happens and sometimes doesn't, which block appreciation of irreversibly wasted opportunities, frustrated potentials, and irrecoverable harms. Put simply, on such a view, the world, at large, cannot get better, or worse, in the same way we now acknowledge it can. Indelible stains on the human record or unprecedented progressions over past oppressions were unthinkable.

Evidently, this also made the extinction of species – and, even more so, of mind – inconceivable. As Saint Bonaventure, again glossing Aristotle around 1200 AD, declared: the cosmos 'cannot exist without men, for in some sense all things exist for the sake of man'.[40] Writing later, Aquinas likewise claimed that it is an 'impossible supposition' to envisage a world without intellects in it.[41]

---

[37] Visser and Williams, *Anselm*, p.48. [38] Nicolaus de Autricuria, *Universal Treatise*, p.40.
[39] Nicolaus de Autricuria, *Universal Treatise*, p.40.
[40] St Bonaventure, *Doctoris seraphici*, vol.II p.254.
[41] Thomas Aquinas, *Disputed Questions*, vol.III p.11.

But, more profoundly, it stultified all sense of meaningful world-historical change – or, large-scale historic shifts for better or worse. Given ours was considered a maximally rational world, God was on pains to maintain its invariant goodness over time, throughout all its shifting permutations. The total '*bonum*' in the universe was considered indestructible and invariable: globally conserved through all interactions and local shifts. Again, limiting possibility to narrowly 'diachronic' usage – as describing that which comes and goes, but only ever as a return of what's come or gone before – means that it can only describe trivial rearrangements rather than irrecuperable losses or genuine novelty.

As Augustine put it, 'variable good' is governed, in the last instance, by 'immutable good'.[42] Meaning that the 'goodness' of created beings can, locally, 'be augmented and diminished'; but, globally speaking, all variations must ultimately average out as 'good because their author is supremely good'.[43] This, again was essentially continuous with the elder, pagan view, which was aptly summed up by Lucretius, who claimed that the 'aggregate of things palpably remains intact', because every death or disappearance is necessarily matched by compensatory birth or renewal:

> no visible object ever suffers total destruction, since nature renews one thing from another, and does not sanction the birth of anything unless she receives the compensation of another's death.[44]

Thus, beyond the implacable and divinely orchestrated countdown to apocalypse, when it came to secular affairs and to human expectation, the medieval outlook – by and large – wasn't too far from the elder view of cycling stasis. Local changes of fate were feasible, but never any shift from the view of the globe: nothing irreversibly destroyed, nothing genuinely novel; always a revolving, never a rupture. Indeed, certain – albeit heterodox – believers happily made pagan eternalism compatible with their Christian faith, such as Siger of Brabant, who in the 1200s professed that nothing is truly unprecedented, such that

> the same species which were, return in a cycle; and so also opinions and laws [and] all other things, although because of the antiquity there is no memory of the cycle of these.[45]

Though deemed heretical, Siger's opinion was not far from the words of *Ecclesiastes*:

---

[42] Augustine, *Contra Adversarium*, bk.I caput.6. All references to Augustine are to the Migne *Opera Omnia* edition.
[43] Augustine, *Enchiridion*, caput.12. [44] Lucretius, *Nature of Things*, p.14, p.10.
[45] Siger of Brabant, *Eternity of the World*, pp.92–93.

> What has been will be again, what has been done will be done again; there is nothing new under the sun.[46]

Indeed, despite the fact that Abrahamic religion taught of a crisp beginning to worldly time, there was no consensus during the Middle Ages about the span from then until the present.[47] Many assumed this duration was, to all intents and purposes, immeasurable: and, thus, readily compatible with Classical teaching that everything humanly achievable must, by necessity, have already been achieved, such that our future could not come to look drastically divergent from its past.

This outlook came to be embodied in the Medieval metaphor of the 'wheel of fortune' – the *Rota Fortunae* made popular by Boethius – whose attraction was adroitly captured by Reinhart Koselleck. The 'circling wheel', Koselleck wrote, 'pointed to the iterability of all occurrence, which in spite of all ups and downs could not introduce anything which was, in principle, new to the world before the time of the Last Judgement'.[48]

But this outlook would begin being dissolved from within by the acidic notion of divine omnipotence. During the later Middle Ages, a string of theologians – both Islamic and Christian – became eager to buttress their conviction that Deity was free to have made our world completely otherwise. This motivated them to develop logical definitions of possibility unmoored and unanchored from all precedent, or, manifestation within time. Indeed, in buttressing Divinity's omnipotence this way, they were led to rejecting that our world exhausts all the ways it could be. This not only evacuated our world of rational structure – where everything is the way it is for a deducible reason – but also opened the door to sensitisation to all the ways our world itself could *become* otherwise, in ways unprecedented. The future began trickled into the frame, eventually becoming a torrent, then a deluge.

Scholasticism made it to the Middle East during the Islamic Golden Age, dating roughly from AD 700 to 1300. Here it blossomed into the teachings of the Muʿtazilite falāsifa (i.e. philosophers) who sought to elucidate the rational necessity of the cosmos along Aristotelian lines. This triggered a counter-reaction from what came to be known as Ashʿarism. The Ashʿarites instead foregrounded God's limitless will, forging a position known as voluntarism. They reproached the Aristotle-inspired encroachments of the Muʿtazilites, for leveraging chains of logical and deductive demonstration over divine decision. In order to exalt God's freedom and omnipotence over such rationalist

---

[46] Ecclesiastes, 1:9. [47] For a brilliant account, see Dal Prete, *On the Edge of Eternity*.
[48] Koselleck, *Futures Past*, p.116.

straightjacketing, they asserted the centrality of divine will in every worldly happenstance and sought to strip the cosmos of any inherent, indwelling rational order.

A prominent example comes from al-Ghazālī and his *Tahāfut al-Falāsifah* of 1095. Here, the Sunni theologian wanted to dismantle the Peripatetic faith in the demonstrability of the connection between cause and effect. As such, he presaged Hume, by saying that the link could not be logically demonstrated.[49] He did this by conjuring up unrealised, yet logically plausible, events that *could* disrupt regular causality.[50] This, in many ways, may have been philosophy's first true conception of catastrophe: a grasp of the purely unprecedented, based upon a higher order acceptance of the disunity of human reason and wider existence.

As such, Islamic and Christian voluntarist theologians moved away from elder definitions of 'contingent' as that which doesn't happen at one moment but does happen another. Instead, it began being deployed to express plausible alternates to what happens at one moment, which thus never have to otherwise come to pass. In so doing, they divorced the concept of possibility from realisation within time, emancipating and liberating its range from the known, familiar, and established course of events.

Though it was already tacit in Augustine's fifth-century proclamation that '*potuit sed noluit*' – that is, there are worlds God could have made, but simply didn't – this new, properly 'synchronic' definition of possibility was first explicitly articulated by Duns Scotus. Writing near the opening of the fourteenth century, Scotus announced:

> I do not call something contingent because it is not always or necessarily the case, but because the opposite of it could be actual at the very moment it occurs.

Scotus here made explicit what was implicit in prior thinkers from al-Ghazālī to Peter Damian, finally consummating a separation of possibility from precedent or eventual manifestation. 'In the late medieval modal theory', writes Hintikka, 'the domain of possibility is accepted as an *a priori* area of conceptual consistency [which is then] divided into different classes of compossible states of affairs of which the actual world is one'. In other words, this new conception explained possibility as delineating a space of conceptual consistency carved up by abstract relations of compatibility, rather than barricaded and gerrymandered

---

[49] Riker, 'al-Ghazālī on Necessary Causality'.
[50] As Kukkonen notes, '[n]o reference to actual existents is necessary' for this argument: 'Only that the mind be capable of grasping a certain set of beings and their properties'. See Kukkonen, 'Mind and Modal Judgement', p.127.

by the fickle horizons of established human experience. Duns Scotus, in other words, had unwittingly provided the logical seedbed of the modern sense of the future as the domain of the entirely unprecedented.

Bewitched by omnipotence, late Medieval theologians started excitedly pondering the ways in which this world could be otherwise. The historian Amos Funkenstein wrote of 'schoolmen [driven] by an almost obsessive compulsion [to] devise orders of nature [different] from the one admittedly existing'.[51] This became ensconced in the popular distinction between '*potentia dei absoluta et ordinata*' – or, between God's absolute power and ordained power – an important bifurcation baptised by Alexander of Hales, to describe the order God upholds *within* this world ('*potentia ordinata*'), as opposed to the totality of what he could make manifest ('*potentia absoluta*').

Buttressing God's freedom in selecting between worlds involved pushing the claim that it is not the way it is for any binding reason nor logical necessity, but is so purely because of arbitrary choice. This eventually led to the claim, articulated most prominently by William of Ockham in the 1300s, that none of the dictates of reason could restrict what reality can be. Motivated by conviction that our mental categories (universals, abstractions, sensations, species, propositional structures) cannot place limits upon what God can do, Ockham imagined existence completely voided of all such mental contents. He did this by deploying the recently strengthened modal logic to put this evacuation into counterfactual relief. That is, arguing that only singulars truly exist, because categorial structures cannot impinge on God's will, Ockham imagined counter-to-fact worlds wherein all such mental categories are procedurally eliminated from the universe, thus abrading reality to its mind-independent kernel. Referring to this as the 'Principle of Annihilation', he imagined universes where everything is removed – '*toto mundo destructo*' – except for one singular object, in pure autonomy of all cognitive generalisations or phenomenal contents.[52] This way, Ockham became the first to properly propose a possible world entirely without intellects within it.

In other words, this was the origin of our modern conception of 'scientific realism' or 'robust mind independence'. It's no coincidence that, writing centuries later, Galileo deployed a similar vocabulary of annihilation, pondering the counterfactual erasure of experience: 'I think that tastes, odours, colours, and so on are no more than mere names so far as the object [is] concerned . . . Hence, if the living creature were removed, all these qualities would be wiped away and annihilated.'[53]

---

[51] Funkenstein, *Theology and the Scientific Imagination*, p.122.
[52] Ockham, *Philosophical Writings*, p.26; Funkenstein, *Theology and the Scientific Imagination*, pp.135–140.
[53] Galileo, *Discoveries & Opinions*, p.274.

Again, by definition, putting reality's mind-independence into relief requires the emancipation of conceptions of possibility from prior human experience. The fact existence will continue without minds like ours can only be articulated counterfactually – that is, insofar as mind like us persist. Hence, why such articulations would have to wait for the late Medieval liberation of possibility from precedent. Ockham's thought experiments – providing the first robust benchmark of mind independence – are the primal scene of all future articulations of our potential extinction.

Much has been written on how this provided the crucible for the birth of modern science.[54] The 'compulsion' of earlier theologians to imagine worlds entirely otherwise than the apparent one was prologue to the later discovery of scientists that the world in fact *is* otherwise than it intuitively appeared.

Indeed, as already hinted at, imagining hypothetical objects entirely outside of all conceptual or experiential relations, as Ockham did, lies at the root of the Early Modern distinction between 'primary' and 'secondary', or mind-independent and mind-dependent qualities. Funkenstein, moreover, notes Galileo's employment of entirely counterfactual scenarios, analogous to Ockham's own, to arrive at the unobservable, and because physically impossible, limit cases (i.e. a frictionless plane) that were required to formulate counterintuitive laws like that of inertia.[55] Oakley and Milton point out the centrality of such thought to the discovery of the modern idea of a 'law of nature' itself.[56] That is, as a parameter that could have been otherwise, in ways blind to the demonstrative approach of Scholasticism, but nonetheless carves up the limits of what can happen within *this* world. Such regularities, being arbitrary and contingent, cannot be rationally deduced from afar, but instead must be investigated by close-up encounters with the world – or, in other words, empirically and inductively.

In this way, modern science can be seen as a fortuitous 'exaptation' of late Medieval obsession with omnipotence. (Where an exaptation is a trait evolved for one purpose, potentially now defunct, fortuitously becomes adaptive for another.)[57] But, aside from generating the intellectual conditions enabling scientific inquiry, it also fomented a growing sense of the future. The two go hand in hand: by enabling the vocabularies required to reverse engineer the

---

[54] Duhem, *Etudes*, vol. II, p.412.
[55] Funkenstein, *Scientific Imagination and Theology*, pp.152–179.
[56] Milton, 'Concept of the "Laws of Nature"'; Oakley, 'Christian Theology and the Newtonian Science'.
[57] This adds another layer of chanciness to the question of the birth of modern science, which may plausibly be leveraged as yet another facet to the so-called Needham Question: or, the riddle of why science developed in Europe rather than China, despite China's more advanced technological development at the time.

nomological structure of the universe, and thus beginning technoscience's accelerating transformation and restructuring of our material conditions, these same vocabularies allowed people to capture the burgeoning sense that genuine change was afoot within one's own lifetime.

Ultimately, in making the world arbitrary, omnipotence stripped it of indwelling reason. Hans Blumenberg called this the '*Ordungsschwund*', or, loss-of-order, that stood at the late Medieval threshold to modernity. The laceration of the old, traditional worldview is what opened the floodgates on the future.

It should be noted here, also, that the late Medieval invention of 'synchronic' possibility, as the selection between simultaneous alternates, may also have been upstream of the development of both of the major modern systems of ethics: utilitarianism and deontology. Ancient and Medieval normative theories were broadly **aretalogical**, or, centred on performing the virtues. This again was often rooted in precedent, or replicating the habits and prior example of admirable people. This, clearly, fits with a 'diachronic' conception of possibility: wherein, as all possibilities eventually come to pass regardless, and can never become forever frustrated, the aggregate of good in the universe over time cannot be affected. Utilitarianism appeals to the idea that the aggregate of good in the cosmos is variable, in potentially unprecedented ways, and teaches that we should select between our actions based on maximising that aggregate. Selecting between alternate actions, some of which may remain forever unrealised, thus plausibly alters that aggregate – in meaningful and lasting ways – because not all possible permutations are guaranteed to come to pass regardless. Deontology, likewise, appeals to a rule of conduct which is meaningful even though it may have never been fully obeyed by any limited, finite being. It is very consciously not rooted in precedent or prior actions. This way, the late Medieval development of new modal logics may have paved the way for, centuries later, the invention of modern systems of ethics too.[58]

What's more, by stripping reality of dependence on mental structures, this inculcated sensitivity to things and events falling beyond all current conceptual categorisation. This lubricated responsivity to the cosmos's non-responsivity to semantic capture and moral expectation: manifesting as new openness to the unexpected, inexplicable, catastrophic, and anomalous. Of course, humans have always dealt with these things, but now new concepts had been developed through which to express and model them.[59]

---

[58] For the influence of new modal logic on Medieval ethical theories, see Knuuttila and Holopainen, 'Conditional Will and Conditional Norms'.

[59] As Brient writes: '[t]he world ordained by God's unbounded will thus no longer presents itself as ordered to human reason and human needs. It is an indifferent and essentially arbitrary reality, indeed, one in which the term "reality" no longer connotes an order of beings or a degree of

In short, by starting to encourage ways of thinking about how the universe *could have been* otherwise than they believed, people started to realise it already *is* otherwise, the realisation of which – snowballing into an undeniable break with the past – lent momentum to a burgeoning sense things *can* and *will become* otherwise in ways unscripted by Deity's predetermination.

Of course, this would not happen overnight. Expectations on the future remained shallow. This was, primarily, because of widespread belief that history was much nearer its end than its beginning. Each generation assumed it might be the last. Jesus himself had told his disciples as much. Indeed, most believers, during the Middle Ages, actively *wanted* the end to come. It would liberate them, they believed, of their Earthly suffering and consecrate the final sorting of Good from Evil. Existence was considered irredeemably alloyed with sin; the only way to purify it was to end it.

In the thirteenth century, towards the end of the Middle Ages, the English polymath Roger Bacon recorded his hopes for the future. He believed 'individuals, cities, and whole regions can be changed for the better' through study and education. But, nonetheless, Bacon still assumed he was living nearer the end, adding that 'it is believed by all the wise that we are not far from the times of the antichrist'.[60]

In 1493, the German writer Hartmann Schedel set out to compile a chronicle of time in its total compendium – stretching from creation to apocalypse. At the end of the book, he left blank pages for his readers to fill in and record history's remaining episodes themselves. The entire volume was roughly three hundred pages long. Schedel left only *six* blank pages for time's remaining episodes.[61]

What's more, again, what unfolded over those remaining blank pages was considered prewritten and predetermined. Even the voluntarists believed that God had selected ours as the best of all possible worlds, wherein value and life are invariant and indestructible qualities, sealed away from vicissitude. Though local change could be affected, the aggregate '*bonum*' of the universe was maintained by God and couldn't be meaningfully altered by humans. 'Mind' and 'life' were not yet subsumed within the Horizon of Contingency as *historical variables*: they were not thought of as emerging from nature nor of as potentially disappearing from it. Instead, all the regions of the premodern cosmos were thought of as populated with spiritual agents – whether angelic or demonic or human – across time and space. The Ptolemaic universe had no unoccupied regions. There was no acknowledgement that nature has an autonomous history, wherein vast regions in time and space can be unpopulated and

---

perfection, but simply comes to mean "that which is the case".' See Brient, *Immanence of the Infinite*, p.66.
[60] Bacon, *Opus Majus*, vol.II, p.417. [61] Schedel, *Liber Chronicarum*.

abiotic. Whether through deity or directionless repeats, an invariant baseline of 'justice' or 'life' was thought of as maintained from start to end.

But then, by good chance, someone discovered how to *measure* chance, thus allowing the unpredictable nature of the future to – finally – become an object of study.

2 Future's Dawn

2.1 Early Modern: That We Can Make the World Otherwise

The historian of ideas Ian Hacking once remarked at how curious it is that, despite the fact almost all other fields of mathematics find their first flourishing in the ancient world, the study of probability remained a 'absent' until the dawn of modernity.[62] There is long-running mystery over probabilism's belated birth: or, why 'probability calculus was so long developing'.[63]

One reason for this, which has yet to be noticed, is the lack of 'synchronic' definitions of possibility prior to Duns Scotus. Conceiving of each throw of the dice as the expression of a wider space of simultaneous alternatives is requisite for grasping probability. Without grasp of 'synchronic' possibility, there could be no such understanding.

Of course, in sortition, divination, casting of lots, and *astragali* (heel bones used as dice), and cleromancy, there is a 'prehistory of randomness' and 'luck epistemics' going back deep into the ancient world.[64] Yet this was apprehended as inscrutable *'fortuna'*, rather than anything formally tractable: until, that is, Gerolamo Cardano's *Liber de Ludo Aleae*, which was written around 1550 and published posthumously in 1663.[65]

In this pathbreaking work, Cardano – a polymath who often resorted to gambling to support himself financially – conducted the 'first real experiments in the mathematics of chance'.[66] Cardano's breakthrough, now deceptively intuitive yet at the root of the entire edifice of the modern world, was in conceptualising each dice-throw *as the expression of a larger set of possibilities*, thus developing the notion of a synchronic possibility space (which Cardano entitled the 'circuit' of the die). In deploying numeral notations to track frequencies within this reference class, Cardano invented the modern field of probability and made the future enumerable. Indeed, by 1654, Pascal – in his correspondence with Fermat – deployed the method to robustly measure future outcomes: computing the cascading number of possible results from an

---

[62] Hacking, *Emergence of Probability*. [63] David, *Games, Gods, and Gambling*, p.36.
[64] David, *Games, Gods, and Gambling*, p.4. [65] Cardano, *Book on Games of Chance*.
[66] Beck and Kewell, *Risk*, p.18.

interrupted game of chance so as to properly allot winnings between players, given likelihoods each player *would* have won *had* the game concluded.[67]

This, in important ways, provided the threshold of 'advanced modernity', leading the way to our modern 'world of speed, power, instant communication, and sophisticated finance'.[68] Indeed, the word '*risk*' first entered the English language throughout the 1600s, percolating first through the professional vocabulary of maritime traders and their insurance underwriters. With the coincident explosion of financial markets, and speculation thereof, futures had become profitable and risk a lucrative business. The future began bleeding into the present, by being carved at the joints – and thus made tangible and tradeable – by Cardano's seismic innovation.

By this time, moreover, worldly time was swelling beyond the bookends prescribed by apocalyptic prophecy. The promised end kept failing to arrive. The more the years continued to accumulate, and the more frustrated their apocalyptic conclusion became, the more there could arrive a growing sense of the *autonomy* of secular history from divine dictatorship. As apocalyptic expectation became increasingly frustrated, that is, worldly time began to seem increasingly untouched by orchestrations from beyond.

This fed into, and was fed by, building conviction that genuinely unprecedented things were being invented and wrought by human agency and activity. History seemed on the move, with human ingenuity – rather than divinity – increasingly with its hands on the rudder. This led some to begin asking, in new ways, *where* they stand within this story. None other than Gerolamo Cardano, writing around 1570, remarked that his position in the generations seems improbable given he appeared to have been born during an uncommonly pacey time of innovation: wherein printing, gunpowder, and the compass had all become widespread in Europe.[69]

But many Renaissance thinkers continued to assume that, though there might be *local* direction to human history – applying *within* one's nation or continent – there may be only aimless cycling and recurrence at the level of the globe. They tended to assume that all novel inventions had already been invented elsewhere and elsewhere, and, by implication, will be *discovered again* should their civilisation be lost or forgotten. Again, there was not yet the evidence sufficient to disprove this: in absence of a global fossil record it remained *underdetermined* as to whether human history had a proper beginning such that it can admit of genuine novelties and irreversible transitions.

---

[67] Devlin, *Unfinished Game*. [68] Bernstein, *Against the Gods*, p.2.
[69] Cardano, *Book of My Life*, pp.89–90.

For example, in 1651's *Leviathan*, Thomas Hobbes spoke of the shift from a warring 'State of Nature' to that of the 'Social Contract'. This might now sound like what we understand as the transition from prehistory to history. We envision a time before which *no* humans, anywhere, practised farming or writing, and a time after which some started. But this wasn't what Hobbes had in mind. He clarified he believed the precivilisational state 'was never generally so, over all the world'.[70]

This betrays assumption that human history – at the level of the globe – could simply represent the cycling of a set of states simultaneously manifested in space, rather than a chronology of genuine firsts and lasts irreversibly punctuating time. A revolving, never a rupture. Regions might slither between states, but, from the global perspective, nothing genuinely novel ever happens or is permanently lost. Every 'civilised' region will have previously been in the 'State of Nature' and every wild region will previously have experienced 'Social Contracts', potentially without limit.

Hobbes's view was far from unorthodox. Many other Early Modern thinkers also understandably erred cautiously when it came to the question of extremities to human history. Writing in his 1513 *Discourses*, Machiavelli again entertained the possibility there have been countless human civilisations, its just the records of them have been 'blotted out by various causes'. Like Plato before him, he endorsed a cyclical view wherein civilisation repeatedly grows to a certain point – that is, 'when human craft and malice have gone as far as they can go' – before everything is destroyed, clearing the way for a reset.[71]

Various commentators remarked that, though new things appeared to be being invented, they couldn't disprove lingering suspicion all these feats hadn't already been innumerably achieved before – by forgotten civilisations, in unknown regions, throughout time immemorial.

Accordingly, by the Early Modern period, the Horizon of Contingency still didn't extend far beyond one's landmass or continent. Nonetheless, this didn't deter growing feeling that human ingenuity – rather than divine dictatorship from the heavens – seemed, increasingly, to be steering history's course. So, too, did a suspicion begin building that time is *open-ended*: that is, that it can take various different tracks, depending on accident and agency flowing from human affairs.

So mused the French polymath Blaise Pascal sometime around 1650: had 'Cleopatra's nose' been different, making her less attractive, then 'the whole face of the earth would have been different'.[72] That is, should Mark Antony *not*

---

[70] Hobbes, *Leviathan*, pp.62–63. [71] Machiavelli, *Chief Works*, vol.I, pp.340–341.
[72] Pascal, *Pensées*, p.162.

have fallen for Cleopatra's distinctive visage, subsequent events would have also been unrecognisable. With this clever quip – bundled with a pleasing pun – Pascal captured an emerging, very modern attitude towards time.

We may be accustomed to such counterfactual conjectures at global scale now; back then, however, they were newfangled. Our grasp of history's contingencies, and of the future's forking paths, has continued growing ever since: an ever-expanding halo of unrealised possibilities fanning out from the merely actual.

Nonetheless, Pascal himself held to the old belief that the space of historical possibility was small enough that everything that can happen already has happened, such that true unprecedented change – in secular affairs – remained unthinkable to him. As he memorably put it, writing in his *Pensées*: 'the nature of man is not to be always going'. In Pascal's eyes, human history evidently 'has its goings and comings'. 'It is the same with human inventions from age to age', Pascal concluded, 'and the same with the goodness and wickedness of the world in general'.[73] In other words, he also believed nothing truly unprecedented happens within worldly history.

Nonetheless, new tools for making the future tractable were being developed. Namely, the mathematics of calculus, developed independently by Isaac Newton and Gottfried Wilhelm Leibniz in the latter 1600s. This allowed the computation of changing rates of change: meaning that anything that can be plotted with a curve – parabolas of orbital paths as much as fluctuations in markets or populations – could suddenly yield to being converted into numbers. These nonlinear processes, formerly intractable to computation, could now be translated into tractable formulas, amenable to retrodiction and prediction. The future yielded to calculation: thanks to offloading our imaginations from imprecise language to the rigour and rule of number. The first triumph of this method was procured by Edmond Halley, who, in 1705, used it to compute the path of the comet that now bears his name. He correctly forecast its future return in 1758, proving long-range numerical prediction of nature's trajectories was possible.

Though its roots go back to the aforementioned Medieval arguments of Duns Scotus and others, Leibniz is also famous for developing the theory of 'possible worlds' in his *Théodicée* of 1710. But, crucially, these evanescent possibilities were hermetically sealed from *our* world. Leibniz, again, believed ours, by necessity, the best. Accordingly, when it came to worldly history, he held a very providentialist view: remarking – after considering some critical counterfactuals – that the 'instants of when things should happen' are, ultimately, 'set by God'.[74]

---

[73] Pascal, *Pensées*, pp.6–7.   [74] See Backus, *Leibniz*, p.173.

What's more, in a fragment penned in 1715, the German polymath set out to gauge the total set of human historic possibilities, with an eye to calculating the interval of time before worldly history resets and repeats itself.

Beginning with the premise that one can 'determine the number of all possible books of a given size composed of meaningful and meaningless words', Leibniz noted this number is finite. Supposing, therefore, that 'a public annual history of the earth can be sufficiently related' in a book containing '100 million letters', he concluded it is 'clear that the number of possible public histories of the earth' is 'limited', because the number of meaningful combinations of 100,000,000 letters is finite. Accordingly, given enough time, human possibilities will 'exhaust' and repeat. Leibniz remarked that the monarchs of his day – from Emperor Leopold I to King Louis XIV – will 'return'.

Going even further, he pronounced that the same calculation can be conducted for our own 'private' histories. Supposing a 'thousand million humans' alive on Earth, he guessed that a book with 100,000,000,000,000,000 characters could exhaustively chronicle every experience of every human over the course of a year. Again, given that the number of meaningful permutations of a book of this length nonetheless remains finite, Leibniz pronounced that every individual life is bound to repeat, down to the smallest minutiae. 'I myself, for example, would be living in a city called Hannover', he mused, 'writing letters to the same friends with the same meaning'.[75]

Leibniz wasn't explicit on the interval of time required for this recurrence to occur, but he was certain it could be meaningfully numbered. Notably, at the time, the entire span of Earth history was often measured in thousands of years, with some outliers admitting the possibility of tens or hundreds of thousands of years.

Indeed, it also remained orthodox to assume the world would last a further several centuries. This sense, of living nearer to history's conclusion than its beginning, affected peoples' sense of ambition and hope for the future ahead. Writing in 1658, Sir Thomas Browne perfectly captured this overriding sentiment. ''Tis too late to be ambitious', he declared:

> The great mutations of the world are acted, or time may be too short for our designes.[76]

But, by this point, in the wake of the Copernican revolution, people could now look beyond the Earth, to other planets, as the places where our history would repeat and recur without limit.

---

[75] Leibniz, 'Apokatastais'.   [76] Browne, *Hydriotaphia*, pp.73–74.

Indeed, Copernicus's revolution made people feel small, but it didn't initially make them feel lonely. Far from it. Responding to the cosmic vastitudes revealed throughout the 1600s, Pascal famously admitted the 'silence of these infinite spaces terrifies me'.[77]

But people forget what else he said. What terrified him wasn't the prospect we were alone, *but the opposite*. He hated the ignominy of being unnoteworthy, or, the idea of countless populated globes that 'know nothing of us' because Pascal assumed all worlds host the same animals Earth houses – down to the 'mites' – such that all Earthly things must cosmically recur 'without end and without cessation'.[78] What alarmed him was how *mundane* this extramundane churn of living globes makes us.

Pascal was far from alone. Confronted by a universe far larger, in space and time, than had previously been permitted by limited imaginations, people simply assumed it lacked limits entirely. Contemporaries, like the Cambridge Platonist Henry More, concluded there will be 'endless' Earths and humankinds. Dizzyingly, he pictured infinite Adams coupling with innumerable Eves. Nothing in infinity is unique, nothing mortal.[79]

Indeed, the belief that the universe is so overflowingly full of living planets made some feel comfortable in proclaiming that the destruction of one must be for the benefit of all, given this provides room for renewal. Retrofitted for the new Copernican cosmology, the old idea of invariant and indestructible 'goodness' – from the level of the cosmic whole – persisted. As the Earl of Shaftesbury wrote in 1711, the idea that all evil is necessarily compensated by equal good, elsewhere or elsewhen, applies to entire planetary systems: whereby 'the evil of one private system is the good of others', such that the destruction of one 'contributes still to the good of the general system', particularly when 'one planetary system ... swallows up another'. The harm to a destroyed system, he continued, 'is not really bad in itself, any more than the pain of cutting new teeth is bad in a system of body which is so constituted that without this episode of pain it would suffer worse by being defective'.[80] Again, historic, irreversible, or unprecedented fluctuations in the aggregate goodness of creation were considered impossible.

So, again, from the perspective of the cosmic whole, there is only constant equilibrium: never any genuine loss or novelty, never any true history. What's more, in such vastitudes, all achievements must necessarily already have been achieved, such that nothing on Earth is truly novel. The Ancient belief – that all

---

[77] Pascal, *Pensées*, p.66.   [78] Pascal, *Pensées*, p.8, pp.60–61.
[79] More, *Democritus Platonissans*, p.12.   [80] Cooper, *Inquiry*, p.10.

historical possibilities have already limitlessly been passed through – had simply receded from other landmasses to other planets.

This way, initially, Copernicus's revolution didn't shrink humanity's ego. It inflated it to cosmic catchments. But figuring out where we find ourselves in time – more specifically, within the chronology of our own planet – slowly but surely, unravelled this.

2.2 Enlightenment: Subsuming Earth within Contingency's Horizon

But then, throughout the 1700s, naturalists began looking to the Earth itself, rather than scripture, to answer the question of the present's location in time. Geology had begun consolidating as a science.

The geological record of superposed strata, each containing different fossils – a ledger of the past – would seem clearly to imply direction. Nonetheless, for a while, naturalists resisted: trying to resolve building evidence of systemic direction into cycles of wider directionlessness and recurrence.

Ahead of digging into the planet, the first geologists assumed they might find proof of nothing really changing throughout Earth's history. They expected remains of everything currently alive on the surface to be located even in the deepest strata. Some predicted that, if we dug to Earth's core, we would find human remains. Thus wrote the French diplomat Benoît de Maillet, speculating in the 1720s:

> If we could dig down to the centre of our globe, [we would see] the remains of several superposed worlds, entire cities, durable monuments, and everything we observe on the surface of the earth, bones of men and animals, some petrified, others not, stones, and marbles, inside which we would find all that occurs in [our world].[81]

Ahead of evidence to the contrary, naturalists assumed the evidences of excavation would eventually reveal a lack of directionality across geologic history. But, when scientists began peeling Earth open, revealing the fossil record's testimony, this isn't what they found. Not only did the eldest strata lack organic remains entirely, they also noticed the skeletons change drastically – becoming less familiar – the deeper you get.

Nonetheless, since at least 1700, scientists had been accumulating evidence of undeniable directionality in Earth's past. In the shape of *vestiges of a beginning*. As early as 1669, geologist Nicholas Steno recorded strata 'free of all [organic] material', implying a period of Earth's history 'when animals and plants had not yet appeared'.[82]

---

[81] de Maillet, *Telliamed*, p.93. [82] Steno, *Original Papers*, p.654.

Moreover, no sign of fossilised humans could be found in the lower beds. Candidates for ancient humans were soon proven to be mistaken, such as one giant salamander fossil, which was briefly mischaracterised as human, by Johann Jakob Scheuchzer in 1726.

By putting a clear *backward stop* on previous human history, alongside implying the recency of all humanity within a much elder Earth system, this meant that it became much more plausible to suggest that not *everything humanly achievable has already been achieved throughout an unbounded past*.

This, in turn, fed into a sense that – rather than being a closed-off repeat of what's come before – the future ahead could be open-ended: *containing novel achievements as well as unprecedented challenges*.

Thus, rather than being made up of directionless returns, resets, and amnesias gyrating through boundless time, human history – as a global whole – could begin to gain an overarching shape: involving determinate firsts and unidirectional transitions between differing states.

As early as 1763, the Russian polymath Mikhail Lomonosov had begun explicitly dismissing the prior attempts of 'Christian chronologists' to gauge the size of Earth's past, before hinting that the testimony of the Earth itself must trump that of the Bible. After all, our planet, Lomonosov explained, is the 'most senior Chronicler of all'. Lomonosov concluded the Earth 'appears to be greater' than previous calculations had indicated.[83]

Having put the question to the rocks, it wasn't long before scientists were widely accepting the Earth had been around for leagues longer than was previously expected. Thousands of year estimates swelled into tens of thousands. Unsurprisingly, it became natural to expect that it might stick around – into the future – for a similar length of time. So, the question was asked: *can geological evidence tell us how long is left ahead for Earth?*

The time was ripe for the first physical theory comprehensively predicting both the past and future of the Earth system. This came from the French polymath Georges Buffon in the 1770s. Theorising the Earth was created from molten matter ejected from the sun, Buffon inferred it would eventually dissipate its internal heat and freeze, killing all life. A molten birth, hurtling inexorably to frozen death.

Retreating to his basement forge in Burgundy, Buffon heated iron balls then measured their cooldown times, before scaling them up to the globe's size. From this, he estimated Earth was around 74,832 years old; that life emerged upon it

---

[83] Lomonosov, *Pervyye osnovaniy*, pp.393–394.

35,983 years ago; and that it would remain habitable for another 93,291 years.[84] (Rounding wasn't yet scientific convention.)

This might seem paltry now, but it was fathoms greater than previous estimates. Indeed, given that time's prior limits seemingly were bursting, some once again saw evidence of limitlessness. Eternity recurred.

Not long after Buffon's investigations, the Scottish geologist James Hutton riposted. He argued that, in explaining Earth's features, only currently observable causes should be conscripted. This was sensible – designed to excise unverifiable explanations from geological science – but Hutton overapplied it wildly.

Hutton became convinced our planet had *never* looked drastically different from how it looks today, nor can it change in future. This keyed into his famous declaration that geologists find 'no vestige of a beginning, no prospect of an end'.[85] Bewitched by the aeons required to sculpt vast mountains and canyons using only mundane processes – like erosion or sedimentation, which work at piecemeal pace – Hutton became convinced the past and future of the Earth system was not just enormously long but, instead, *limitlessly long*. He applied this to the future as much as the past. Sometimes hailed as the 'discoverer of deep time', nothing could be further from the truth. Hutton was drunk on boundlessness, not deep time.

This way, eternity briefly recurred: by ceding ground and receding from human history to the mists of geological time. But, despite Hutton's efforts, Buffon's view – that Earth's biography has determinate bookends in time – slowly won the day, as evidence of an epoch before all life became undeniable.

The habitable planet had thus gained a definitive beginning and a bounded future: providing the ambit, the extremities, within which human history could be understood as unfolding, and as unfolding in a way that – *because of the boundedness* – could admit of persistence, genuine firsts, and irreversible losses. Eventually, this would come to replace the default assumption that global human history unfolds as a limitlessly reversible and retraceable meandering through time immemorial.

Because of this, there emerged a sense of time ahead, bounded yet capacious, within which novel things could be achieved and persistently accumulated. But, by the same token, this also meant that *what might be lost*, in the event of planetary disaster, could also begin to become articulable.

---

[84] A completionist, Buffon even calculated the periods of habitability for all the other planets in the Solar System, assuming them to also be occupied by life. See Buffon, *Histoire naturelle*, vol. XXXI, p.404.

[85] Hutton, 'Theory of the Earth', p.304.

Given the new knowledge won by geology, the Horizon of Contingency had expanded to circumscribe the entire planet, bequeathing it the temporal bookends within which history's contingencies could gain bite, insofar as there was no longer a guarantee all outcomes would come to pass regardless. Though Duns Scotus, back around 1300, had invented his logic of possible worlds in order to say how things could have been otherwise, this same logic was now being leveraged to reveal how things – at planetary scale – can become dramatically otherwise.

2.3 Evolution: Subsuming Species within Contingency's Horizon

Nonetheless, contingency didn't yet enter the picture. In 1777, Buffon himself once speculated what would happen if all life was wiped out globally:

> let us suppose for a moment that ... all currently existing individuals ... should be stricken with death at the same instant.[86]

He imagined that, after this, there 'could not fail' to be reproduced 'a new living Nature'. Furthermore, he made explicit that he thought:

> This replacement of living Nature [would soon exhibit] the same general plan of organisation and the same varieties in the particular forms.[87]

Why did Buffon assume this? The answer is because there was not yet any clear understanding of how species originate, such that there could be no grasp of what precisely is lost when their populations are destroyed to the last member. There was no consensus that, once lost, they are gone *forever*.

Many assumptions regarding origination of species – prior to Darwin – actively obstructed grasping this. Going back centuries, one prevalent theory – affirmed also by Buffon – held that each species 'pre-exists' all its manifestations, as invisible 'seeds', diffused through the atmosphere. These were assumed 'indestructible': i.e. they always have existed and always will. All that was needed, it was believed, were welcoming conditions and the 'seeds' would simply germinate into fully adapted species, without need of parents.

This means that a species can persist even if it has *no* living members. Such a theory makes the origin of species effortless, in that such origination lacks any timespan or stringency of circumstances, because it bypasses all the steps we now know are required – to be traced through, from simpler to less simple forms – in order to forge a complex lifeway.

---

[86] Buffon, *Histoire naturelle,* vol.XXXIII, p.359.
[87] Buffon, *Histoire naturelle,* vol.XXXIII, p.363.

There's no multiplicity of prior states the world needs to have passed through for species to pass from inexistence to existence; the corollary of this is assuming that, if a population dies out here and now, it's hard to see what would obstruct it from later reappearing elsewhere.

In the earlier 1700s, de Maillet rallied this theory to explicitly deny the irreversibility of extinction:

> There are few countries in which characteristic species of animals [have] not disappeared. [But these] species which we know have … vanished from Earth, certainly survive, [as] their seeds still occur in the air surrounding it and therefore could reappear again any day.[88]

As late 1819, the influential German biologist Lorenz Oken conjectured that humanity was first generated in such a way: gestated from 'slime' in sea shallows, without descending from prior forms. He even speculated, sincerely, as to how the first generation of children fed and fended for themselves, given there were no parents to show them the ropes.[89]

Put simply, belief in the spontaneous generation of complex things, without the need of any prior histories, neuters the consequences of their eradication: because there's no stringency of states, the universe must retrace to produce identical, or similarly complex, classes of entities again.

Falsifying the presupposition that annihilated species could return required the testimony of the fossil record: wherein lost fauna never return. And, again, not just on one landmass or continent but spanning them. This, however, is precisely what scientists had been piecing together from the early 1700s onwards.

By 1800, the scientific community accepted the reality of irreversible extinction.[90] A few decades later, sequence started to be accepted: a succession of fauna over time, with earlier forms more unfamiliar and later forms more closely resembling those extant today. Naturalists hypothesised an initial 'Era of Fish', then an 'Era of Reptiles', followed by today's 'Era of Mammals'.

Nonetheless, the causes behind this faunal succession remained unclear. Many simply assumed that each era's fauna were *'fresh creations'*: that they aren't descended from the creatures of prior periods, nor are related to them in any 'material' way.

Some, as late as the 1840s and 1850s, argued that *not a single organism* has ever passed offspring between past epochs. They held that, each time, the Earth is wiped entirely clean of life – by some cataclysm – before entirely unrelated,

---

[88] de Maillet, *Telliamed*, pp.228–230. [89] Rupke, 'Neither Creation nor Evolution'.
[90] See Moynihan, 'Existential Risk and Human Extinction'.

novel animals are simply 'called into existence', entirely from scratch, whether by divine intervention or nature's inherent creativity.[91]

As late as the 1840s, Louis Agassiz – an immensely influential biologist – was still insisting that life's succession proceeds this way and 'is not the consequence of a direct lineage between the faunas of different ages'. 'There is nothing like parental descent connecting them', he ordained.[92]

Today, we now recognise that the smallest possible number of steps required to assemble a complex mammal from unorganised matter – entirely from scratch and without the help of pre-existing parents – is something *on the order of four billion years of uninterrupted evolution*. That is, the *shortest pathway* to the biosphere's current richness demands an ancestry billions of years deep.

But, if you don't see this, assuming contrarily something as exquisite as an entire ecosystem can simply be forged 'afresh', each time the world is wiped clean, it's much harder to see the weight of what might be lost in planetary disaster.

We now know species are *historical entities* – they cannot simply spawn independently of myriad prior states of the world holding true. This is why, should they be lost, they cannot effortlessly reappear. It was, of course, Darwin who allowed the world to see this. With his 1859 *Origin of Species*, he demonstrated that complex lifeways are only ever wrought by stringent, long-winding histories. Accordingly, members of a species cannot spawn anywhere, anytime, effortlessly, because they need a connection to a shared past, in the form of parents and countless ancestors.

Darwin was himself conclusive:

> When a species has once disappeared from the face of the Earth, we have reason to believe that the same identical form never reappears ... for the link of generations has been broken.[93]

Organic complexity thus becomes a kind of *stock*, built only over time: it doesn't just require one prior state to hold, it requires myriads, in unbroken chains of cumulative inheritance, stretching back eons. Without the 'shortcut' of already procreating parents, there is no way of skipping these steps.

Solely upon apprehending this could it become truly apparent how *historically consequential* any destruction or loss of that planetary stock might be. Though it would take a few more generations for adherents of Darwin's theory to truly realise what this entails concerning the scope of the contingency of every Earthly species. So, in the years following *Origin of Species*, life's

---

[91] Agassiz, *Iconographie*, p.8. [92] Agassiz, *Outlines*, vol.1, p.417.
[93] Darwin, *Origin*, p.343.

lineages themselves began being subsumed within the Horizon of Contingency: as products of events which didn't have to have happened, as therefore contingent and definitively destructible.

This was a far cry from the Medieval worldview, wherein the universe could not suffer a single loss or annihilation, insofar as this would denude the 'complement of good' housed within it.

3 Contingency Unbound

3.1 Thermodynamic: Subsuming the Sun within Contingency's Horizon

But how much longer did life have left? What further development might be possible? Answering this question involved estimating how long it had taken for life to arrive at its current grandeur and diversity, so as to gauge how much further diversification could be cumulated in the time left ahead.

By the mid 1800s, due to the birth of thermodynamics – the mathematics which models the flow of energy and heat – the question of Earth's future habitability was, by now, understood to hinge upon the sun's remaining lifespan. As John Tyndall put it in 1863:

> Look at the integrated energies of our world – the stored power of our coalfields; our winds and rivers; our fleets, armies, and guns. What are they? They are all generated by a portion of the sun's energy.[94]

So, how long was left? Mid-century, physicists provide the first hypothetical model for how the sun was formed and produces its heat. Thermodynamic calculation was leveraged to estimate how long the sun had already been burning, as well as to forecast how many years of sunlight might be left.

At this time, however, it was uncertain how our star produces its outpouring. Scientists had already decided it couldn't be combusting, like a gigantic coal, since a cinder the size of our sun would burn itself up far more rapidly than seemed plausible. This jarred with the timescales required to explain geological features on Earth.

Long before anyone alive had dreamed of liberating atomic energy, various explanations were proposed, assuming stars shine through some mechanical process. The most popular was that the sun produces its heat by languorously collapsing under its own vast weight. Grinding on its own matter as it compacts, outputting heat and light as the result.[95]

A proponent of this model, William Thomson produced the first prediction for the future output of the sun in 1854. He confidently announced:

---

[94] Tyndall, *Heat*, p.448. [95] See Kragh, 'The Source of Solar Energy'.

> Sunlight cannot last as at present for 300,000 years.[96]

By end of 1800s, physicists had, by and large, converged upon an estimate in the low tens of millions for Earth's habitable future. As the US spectroscopist Charles Augustus Young relayed in 1881:

> the sun [won't] continue to give sufficient heat to support life on the earth ... for ten million years from the present time.[97]

The past and future of *the whole* Solar System had thus become large but bounded, and, thus, subsumed within the Horizon of Contingency. The fates and fortunes of life within this zone were beginning to be acknowledged as irreversible and open to playing out, permanently, in different ways.

Nonetheless, many found the extent of future ahead, for life on Earth, dispiriting. Forecasts of 10,000 further years were admittedly much more commodious than Buffon's earlier estimates, not to mention those of earlier Christians. However, in the century since Buffon, the sense of life's unexplored potentials had grown – largely thanks to Darwin's theories.

What's more, the theory that the sun produces heat via collapsing on itself led physicists to conclude the ratio of 'past spent' to 'future ahead' was unforgiving. If it had started life as a diffuse cloud, our star – now relatively compact and dense – seemed at an advanced, geriatric stage of life's arc. In the 1892 words of Robert S. Ball:

> It seems that the sun has already dissipated about four-fifths of the energy with which it may have originally been endowed.[98]

Accordingly, the placement of the present placement of 'now' – relative to established past and potential future – had returned to a position similar to that of the early Christians.

This predicament seemed depressing to many. There was a sense evolution had come thus far, but didn't have time to go much further. People assumed life had passed its prime: that the future would be populated by increasingly simple life forms, withering on a diet of dwindling sunlight.

So, as the 1800s closed, there was a belief there wasn't time nor available energy to see much more development, nor to care *too urgently* about the longer-run ramifications of our actions. A freezing death awaited in the not-too-distant future (see Figure 1).

But, then, as the 1900s opened, an entirely new force of nature was discovered: blowing the ceiling off all previous upper bounds on the future. Having coined the

---

[96] Thomson, 'Mechanical Energies of the Solar System', p.78.   [97] Young, *The Sun*, p.276.
[98] Ball, 'How Long Can the Earth Sustain Life?' p.490.

Surpris: par le froid, la dernière famille humaine a été touchée au doigt de la Mort, et bientôt ses ossements seront ensevelis sous le suaire des glaces éternelles...

Figure 1 Charles Joseph Mettais, 'The Last Couple on Earth', depicting the final human family succumbing to global cold. From C. Flammarion, L'Astronomie Populaire (1880).

word '*radio-activité*', Marie Curie successfully isolated radium in 1902. Not long after, she proved that the element expels energy without itself losing heat. Radioactive atoms, she showed, were tiny furnaces. This reveals a titanic, previously unacknowledged, wealth of energy is locked up within mundane matter.

Moreover, given the extreme length of decay rates, it also provided the first reliable way of accurately measuring physical processes, past and future, stretching into the many billions of years. Timescales couldn't help but expand.

Immediately, scientists started postulating that radioactive power somehow fuels the stars. Rather than languidly collapsing on itself, the sun now seemed like a self-heating furnace. Almost overnight, this drastically expanded estimates on upper bounds for solar lifespan, and, therefore, also for future habitability on Earth. As early as September of 1903, the geophysicist George Darwin celebrated Curie's 'unexpected' discovery of this 'new source of energy'. If the Sun powers itself by 'liberating atomic energy', he conjectured, rather than mere gravitational collapse, then we may have to expand the 'cosmical time-scale' by 'some such factor as ten or twenty'.[99]

By 1907, the physicist Ernest Rutherford concurred, announcing we can expect solar 'brilliancy' for orders of magnitudes more than Kelvin's considerations of no 'more than 12 million years and probably much less'. Curie's 'new source of heat', Rutherford wrote, probably suffices to power the 'sun for a longer period', thus vouchsafing a much greater 'time for habitation of our globe'.[100] By 1920, prominent physicist Arthur Eddington was venturing that our sun, powered by subatomic reservoirs, would be able to 'maintain its output of heat for 15 billion years' more. To hammer home his point, he referred to the gravitational theory of Kelvin and Helmholtz as a 'corpse'.[101]

Rather than living in a geriatric world, humankind suddenly seemed youthful. Within a generation, peoples' sense of where they find themselves in terrestrial time had flipped: from believing they were living nearer the end, towards thinking they could be living during the dawn. Scientist quickly noted this means we should be more careful, remaining alert to the ways present action can scar or damage the expanding future. The Illinoisan geologist Thomas Chrowder Chamberlin put it best, proclaiming in 1903:

> We have grown up in the belief that the earth [is] plunging [to] a final winter in the near future. Quite at variance with this, [we now know that our planet] offers a fair prospect of fitness for habitation for ages yet to come. If this be true, it is eminently fitting that [humanity] should give a due measure of thought to the ulterior effects of its actions.[102]

As the twenties roared, timescales continued to boom. By this time, physicists and cosmologists were predicting tens of billions of years of future habitability on Earth, some even a trillion. In the decades since, this has progressively been slashed downward, as it discovered our sun will expand, rather than contract, as it ages and was became understood how this expansion will interact with Earth's

---

[99] Darwin, 'Radio-Activity and the Age of the Sun', p.496.
[100] Rutherford, 'Some Cosmical Aspects of Radioactivity'.
[101] Eddington, 'The Internal Constitution of Stars', p.354–355.
[102] Chamberlin, 'Soil Wastage', pp.5–6.

atmosphere. Nonetheless, it remains testament to how much peoples' sense of the possibilities and potentials of the future was expanding during the early 1900s.

But, during the 1930s, thanks to the work of Lise Meitner and others, understanding of nuclear fission coalesced. This led, ultimately, to the fateful uncorking of atomic energy, which, in turn, led to the development of atomic weapons: terrifying in their destructive potentials. Suddenly, the radically expanded prospect revealed by nuclear physics was being put in jeopardy by that very same force. As Freud put, already in 1931:

> Men have gained control over the forces of nature to such an extent that with their help they would have no difficulty in exterminating one another to the last man.[103]

Yet, just as the Ancients and Early Moderns could point beyond their own landmass, in order to gesture beyond history's horizon to the region wherein things will comfortably repeat and recoup, so too ponderers in the early 1900s point *beyond* the Solar System – to other stars and systems – so as to conjecture that regardless of humanity's fate here on Earth, there will always and forever be abundant 'other humanities' spread throughout the limitless cosmos. This provided assurance, as well as insurance.

This is why, as the French astronomer Camille Flammarion emotively put it in 1868 the starry expanses are 'the future regions of our immortality' as the 'number of our body doubles is infinite in time and space'.[104] Later, in 1888, he reiterated this point, claiming that our sun will one day 'disappear to leave room for other systems of worlds, other suns, other earths, other humanities, other souls, – successors in universal and eternal history'. This, essentially, was a return to earlier, Lucretian views: of a universe unlimited in space and time, wherein everything is a repeat or return. (As Lucretius himself had said, writing nearly a millennium before, there will always be, 'in other parts of the universe', worlds 'inhabited' by 'many different peoples'.)[105] For Flammarion's part, he continued his argument, declaring:

> Such are the destinies of the Earth and of all the worlds. Must we conclude that, in these successive ends, the universe will one day be nothing more than an immense and black tomb? No, otherwise, since eternity past, it would already be so.[106]

Flammarion's compatriot, the socialist Louis-Auguste Blanqui put this position strongest. In his 1872 *L'Eternité par les astres*, he pronounced:

---

[103] Freud, *Civilization and Its Discontents*, p.112.   [104] Flammarion, *La pluralite*, p.314.
[105] Lucretius, *Nature of Things*, p.62.   [106] Flammarion, *Astronomie populaire*, p.104.

> All the beautiful things that our world will see, our future descendants have already seen them, are seeing them now and will see them always, of course, in the form of doubles that preceded them and will follow them.

These 'doubles', he clarified, are 'body-double' in 'flesh and bone, even in trousers and vest, in crinoline and chignon'. He also added that this means 'there is no progress', cosmically speaking, but only 'vulgar reissues' and 'repetitions'.[107]

Such belief was attached to related assumptions about the origination of life itself. Indeed, many theorised that in a cosmos without a beginning, life itself also need not be historical, in the sense of never having properly 'originated' anywhere or anywhere, such that it also can never properly have an 'end'.

This took the form of the theory of 'panspermia', popular during the decades straddling 1900, which argued that life doesn't originate or emerge – at a certain place or time – but simply circulates unendingly from system to system, and always has done, in the form of 'cosmic spores' or 'astroplankton'. As the German biologist August Weismann stated in 1881, the corollary of panspermia is that

> life can only arise from life, and has always so arisen, [and so] organic beings are eternal like matter itself.[108]

Moreover, panspermia meant that, on average and over time, the amount of life in the eternal cosmos will remain invariant. One planet may die, another may be germinated, but these average out in the longest term. The Swedish astronomer Svante Arrhenius made this clear in his 1908 *World in the Making*, proclaiming that this means organic evolution 'can continue in an eternal cycle, in which there is neither beginning nor end, and in which life may exist and continue forever and undiminished'.[109] Again, this was not a far cry from elder, Medieval notions of a world wherein all the losses and gains, all victories and defeats, equal out into an historically invariant aggregate of 'value'.

3.2 Cosmical: Subsuming the Universe within Contingency's Horizon

Accordingly, even though Darwin's theory made it wildly improbable, people could still seek immortality for our species in the stars. Given an eternity of chances, even the most unlikely confluence of conditions will innumerably repeat. Hence, why, in the 1929 words of one Nobel-winning physicist, there will always be, somewhere, an 'Earth' – 'it matters not which' – upon which

---

[107] Blanqui, *Eternity by the Stars*, pp.150–154. [108] Weisman, 'Ueber die Daeur des Lebens'.
[109] Arrhenius, *Worlds in the Making*, p.211.

'some billion years hence the development of man still may be going on'.[110] In an eternal, infinite universe, such resurrection is inevitable. Such a thought was comforting, some began remarking, given that humans had begun messing with atoms.

But then the Universe *itself* started gaining bookends in time. Peering into the world's largest telescope, around 1920, Edwin Hubble noticed something bemusing about other galaxies outside our Milky Way. They are flinging away from us, at quickening pace the further away they get. Our Universe is expanding.

Extrapolating backwards, this implied an explosive beginning. Inferring forwards, it implied a rarefied end, with matter and energy eventually centrifuging into nihility. The Universe – as one giant physical whole – was gaining a beginning and end.

The Belgian physicist Georges Lemaître pieced it all together first. He theorised the Universe was birthed by titanic detonation. In 1931, Lemaître proposed our cosmos isn't unborn and undying, but can be compared to a fireworks display.[111] Standing on a 'well-chilled cinder', we peer into space, witnessing the explosion's ember-scattering aftermath. In 1946, Lemaître published a book summarising his vision. Poetically, he wrote:

> The evolution of the universe can be compared to a display of fireworks that has just ended: some few red wisps, ashes and smoke. Standing on a well-chilled cinder, we see the slow fading of the suns, and we try to recall the vanished brilliance of the origin of worlds.[112]

Just three years later, speaking on BBC Radio, the astronomer Fred Hoyle absentmindedly referred to Lemaître's theory as the 'Big Bang'. The name stuck.

It wasn't long before this radical theory started winning over influential physicists, and it wasn't much longer than that until they started extruding its entailments for life in general. The Russian-American physicist George Gamow was spelling it out, already, in 1941:

> Not so long ago, one of the favorite explanations of the appearance of life on our planet was the [panspermia] hypothesis. [But this] becomes rather senseless in the light of modern knowledge ... that the stars themselves are not eternal and were born ... This 'physical creation of the universe' must have taken place during the epoch preceding the formation of our Earth and other planetary systems, and since it is obvious that at that time *no life could exist anywhere in the universe*, the problem of the origin of life has to be faced anew.[113]

---

[110] Millikan, 'When the Sun Goes Cold', p.141.   [111] Lemaître, 'Evolution of the Universe'.
[112] Lemaître, *Primeval Atom*, p.78.   [113] Gamow, *Biography of the Earth*, p.155.

Around the same time, there were various important breakthroughs in origin-of-life research. Through the 1920s and 1930s, Russian biochemist Aleksandr Oparin had become the first to pose life's origin as a *specifically historical* question. Previously, it was assumed either that life didn't originate and simply eternally circulated (i.e. panspermia) or that it was constantly emerging from non-living matter (i.e. spontaneous generation). Both theories remove any significant factor of time.

Oparin reframed the problem by asking whether radically different atmospheric conditions in Earth's past could have allowed gradual build-up of organic molecules from inorganic compounds. This, innovatively, brought history back into the picture: the reason we don't see life emerging from non-life today is because these special conditions no longer hold.

Following Oparin's conjectures, in 1952 the American chemist Stanley Miller replicated these conjectured young-Earth conditions in the lab, managing to synthesise organic monomers.[114] This leant credence to 'abiogenesis': the idea that life arose from non-living matter, potentially only once in the past, through a cumulative process. This new theory implied life was not some timeless, and thus universal, phenomenon, but the product of a specific confluence of past events.

Back in the earlier 1900s, it was still assumed – as one science writer summarised in 1920 – that we ought to 'expect life to arise wherever the conditions exist'.[115] But, as the decades dragged on, even this position became less surefooted. Slowly, a new suggestion gained prominence: that life's emergence, on Earth, may have been unlikely, an event birthed by luck or lottery. By the 1960s, writers were remarking we might do well to begin viewing life's emergence 'in terms of probability and chance rather than as the outcome of aim and effort'.[116] But, as far back as 1933, the biochemist Frederick Gowland Hopkins was already stressing that many of his colleagues were in agreement that 'life's advent' on Earth might stand as one of the 'most improbable' events in the 'history of the Universe'.[117]

This began to imply that life, rather than being cosmically abundant across time and space, is a product of historical happenstance: the result of a series of flukes. Thus, it might well be cosmically scarce, perhaps even unique. Accordingly, what happens to Earth's life in the future could no longer so surely seem a matter of triviality or warranting nonchalance.

Further, in 1964, two American astronomers – Arno Allan Penzias and Robert Woodrow Wilson – accidentally discovered the Cosmic Microwave

---

[114] Miller and Urey, 'Organic Compound Synthesis'.
[115] McCabe, *The End of the World*, p.129.   [116] Kapp, *Toward a Science*, p.102.
[117] Gowland Hopkins, 'Some Chemical Aspects of Life', p.2.

Background Radiation. This is a faint hiss, coming at us from all angles. It is the omnipresent reverberation of the universe's pyrotechnic beginning. This was received as overwhelming evidence for the so-called Big Bang Theory. It was tantamount to confirmation that the observable cosmos itself must have had a beginning and is finite in space.

This had subtle, yet profound, ramifications on our view of life's place within the wider cosmos. The American anthropologist Loren Eiseley put it best in 1953:

> Fifty years ago, there was a widely held belief in the infinity of time. While old star systems burned out and died, new systems emerged. ... The idea of an eternal universe allowed the possibility of the spores of life drifting from the wreckage of burned-out systems to systems beginning anew, and an infinity of time in which man might arise again and again.

Continuing, he stated:

> But we have now acquired the growing suspicion that we live in an expanding universe which had an incredible beginning and threatens to have an even more fantastic end. Time, in the only sense we can know it, is limited ... the same life does not come again, the same hands will never twice build the golden cities of this world. The time stream, the on-pouring, whatever we may call it, is far more original than this.[118]

In other words, in a universe with a beginning and a finite lifespan – no matter how large – it's no longer feasible to fall back on the assumption that, regardless of what happens here and now, there *always* be other humanities and biospheres identical to our own, elsewhere and elsewhen. So, should we destroy any species – including ourselves – here and now, then these unique and unrepeatable products of terrestrial history are likely gone, from the entire universe, forever after.

Which is to say, the Horizon of Contingency had ballooned to cosmic catchments. Yet still, there remained one stubborn assumption obstructing full appreciation of the practical force of this realisation on our orientation towards our own future.

3.3 Extinction: Subsuming Sapience within Contingency's Horizon

Going all the way back to Darwin, there persisted overriding assumption that something sapient was the inevitable outcome of macroevolution. Thus, if humanity died out here and now, then something like it would eventually re-emerge – and resume sapience's project, so to speak – on Earth or elsewhere.

---

[118] Eiseley, 'Is Man Alone?'

Darwin himself had been convinced that, in the main, species predominantly are pushed to extinction by their more adaptive descendants and competitors. In other words, it is a question of *bad design*, not *bad luck*.

For this reason, Darwin himself downplayed the role of planetary cataclysms that could decimate indiscriminately, wiping out even the most 'successful' lineages. He maintained that what looked like mass extinction events were just distortions of our incomplete view on the fossil record.

This underwrote a thoroughly progressivist view of macroevolution, where, in Darwin's deeply influential words:

> as natural selection works solely by and for the good of each being, all corporeal and mental endowments will tend to progress toward perfection.[119]

Of course, 'perfection' was here assumed to resemble something rational and humanoid. In an 1860 letter, Darwin went so far as to conjecture that rational beings would always inevitably re-evolve after being extinguished 'if every Vertebrate were destroyed throughout the world', except the humble reptiles, he conjectured, then, after 'millions of ages', they would inevitably 'become highly developed on a scale equal to mammals' – 'possibly more intellectual'.[120]

Most of Darwin's followers, for much of the 1900s, followed this lead. There was widespread assumption that extinction largely befell *decrepit* or *spent* lineages of life; such that, despite detours and delays, all macroevolution inexorably tends towards humanoid perfection.

Extinction was self-servingly assumed to only ever befall the *deserving*. This was applied particularly – sometimes with surprising spite – to the dinosaurs. Well into the century, the stereotypical view was that they died out due to sluggishness or stupidity, and were thus mercifully pruned from the world, so that we 'superior' and 'intellectual' mammals could take over. As one paleontological artist put it in 1946:

> the world was to grow away from these slow-moving dunces, and little warm-blooded beings, furry, alert and aggressive, were to supersede them.[121]

Though some dissented, it nonetheless remained common to assume that something like humanity was the inevitable outcome of macroevolution, here and elsewhere in the cosmos. At the 1969 centenary of *Origin of Species*, one scientist confidently pronounced the following:

> Hence, I see the development of higher types of mammals and, to some extent, of a being like man as necessitated.[122]

---

[119] Darwin, *Origin*, p.489.   [120] Darwin, *Life and Letters*, vol.II, p.344.
[121] Knight, *Life through the Ages*, p.20.   [122] Tax, *Evolution after Darwin*, vol.III, pp.149–151.

Unsurprisingly, such assumption was applied not only to Earth's future but also to planets beyond our Solar System. During the Cold War (indeed, *because* of the Cold War), it was often stated that, should humanity atomically self-destruct on Earth, there would at least be other rational beings, elsewhere, who would be able to give the world-riddle another shot. As the Hungarian essayist Arthur Koestler put it, musing in 1953,

> Perhaps, when they read about the latest hydrogen bomb tests, people are more aware than they admit to themselves, of the possibility that human civilisation may be approaching its end. And together with this may go a dim, inarticulate suspicion that the human race may be a biological misfit doomed to extinction like the giant reptiles of an earlier age. Some apocalyptic intuition of this kind may be one of the reasons for the sudden interest in life on other stars.[123]

Bluntly, calling humanity 'necessitated' is the opposite of accepting that it could easily – contingently – suffer a similar fate as the dinosaurs. In general, assuming extinction only happens to 'the deserving' was not only self-serving but it also obstructed sensitivity that it can befall lifeways which could *otherwise* have gone on, flourishing and diversifying.

But such a view would be dismantled in the latter decades of the century. As the 1980s opened, conclusive evidence began building, implying the dinosaurs were decimated by a chancy asteroid collision. Having been downplayed since Darwin – to the point of investigation being stymied – this went on to reveal the huge importance of chance, contingency, and mass extinction in shaping life's history.[124]

Suddenly, it became highly plausible the dinosaurs didn't die from 'bad genes', but from sheer 'bad luck': a comet, after all, cannot be rationalised away as the handmaiden of progress nor as adaptation's invisible hand.

This had three, profound but subtle, consequences. First, the new view implied that, should the asteroid not have chanced upon Earth, we cannot assume that anything humanoid would have ever emerged. Or, in the 1983 words of the Polish polymath Stanisław Lem, none of us would be here if there hadn't been, 66 million years ago, 'a catastrophe in the form of an enormous, 3.5-to-4-trillion-ton meteorite'. We are, Lem concluded, the fluke product of the 'roulette wheels that are galaxies'.[125]

Second, by demonstrating how the marks of contingency cast their legacies deep through evolutionary history, the impact hypothesis made much more salient the impacts of present-day human action upon life's further future.

---

[123] Koestler, 'Boredom of Fantasy', pp.891–892. [124] See Alvarez, *Crater of Doom*.
[125] Lem, *One Human Minute*, pp.92–93.

Suggestions that we are altering everything to come – in ways which wouldn't otherwise have come to pass – gained more force.

Tellingly, it was precisely around the same time, in the 1980s, that prominent scientists – such as Richard Leakey – first began asserting that we are living during the '*sixth mass extinction*', triggered by human activities and decisions.[126]

For Leakey and others, it was clearly a recognition of the newfound role of *contingence*, in previous mass extinctions, which led him to insisting we take responsibility today. Indeed, prior generations of scientists – going back to Darwin – had made excuses for anthropogenic ecocide, explaining it away as part of nature's inexorable search for the fittest.

Imputing culpability for a wrongdoing, after all, assumes that things could have played out differently had the wrongdoer acted differently. But long-held progressivist assumption had enabled prior intellectuals to pardon anthropogenic extinction as progress's handmaiden. Again, ahead of strong contrary evidence, people have historically proven less that readily willing to extend the notion of genuine contingency far beyond human affairs, up to evolutionary and planetary scales. But the impact evidence forced such extension.

Third, and finally, the new view of mass extinction toppled any residual assurance that an animal as 'adaptive' as *Homo sapiens* won't be succumbing to extinction any time soon. It demonstrated that even the most dominant and preeminent animals can perish: leaving no progenitors nor hope of a 'replay', entirely due to lottery or folly, rather than bad design or decrepitude.

For these reasons, its probably not a mere coincidence that, as Stephen Jay Gould liked to point out, research into the K-Pg impact dovetailed into the first serious research on the severity of nuclear winter:

> A recognition of the very phenomenon [i.e. impact winter] that made our evolution possible by exterminating the previously dominant dinosaurs ... might actually help to save us from joining those magnificent beasts in contorted poses among the strata of the earth.[127]

It also no coincidence that the evolutionists who pioneered this new view of macroevolution were also amongst the first to apply the techniques of *computer simulation* to their field. This included the aforementioned Stephen Jay Gould – who communicated ideas of evolutionary contingency to wide audiences – alongside David M. Raup. Raup, in particular, had established himself, in the 1960s, by applying computer techniques to show how the shells of *actual* seasnails occupy only a small region within a much wider space of *merely*

---

[126] Leakey and Lewin, *The Sixth Extincion*.   [127] Gould, 'Sex, Drugs, Disasters'.

possible morphologies. Raup called this the 'morphospace': expressing all the living forms that could have been, but simply aren't.

By the end of the millennium, the Horizon of Contingency had subsumed everything about humanity. Though he didn't quite explicate it himself, and it took subsequent evolutionists like Gould to draw it fully out, this was one of the profounder upshots of what Darwin discovered. Species are forged by unrepeatable histories, which tether them, in time and space, to their place – and thus planet – of origin. All of Earth's life forms are unique to Earth, just as island creatures are never found anywhere else, unless their ancestors migrated there. Therefore, bracketing the possibility of interstellar migration, should any species be wiped out or lost from Earth, here and now, we can be sure it will never be returning, anywhere, forever after. Extinction isn't just an absence applying to all future moments of time, but to the entire spatial cosmic volume. These are the stakes of what happens next, during the age of the Sixth Mass Extinction.

4 Conclusion: Deep Possibility in the Non-Ergodic Universe

We now know we live in a universe where irreversibility has bite at the largest scales. We now know the extinction, of any terrestrial species, will be cosmically permanent. But there is another upshot of this outlook. By making history cosmic, *there arrives the possibility of making cosmic history*. Or, in other words, in a universe that is thoroughly historical – one that admits of non-ergodic processes at the largest scales – it is at least plausible that biological or intelligent agency, or whatsoever sort, may one day impart some kind of meaningfully lasting influence upon its cosmic environment.

For in an eternal universe, this – if possible – would have already happened, and we would live amongst the results. But, instead, the galaxies seem radically azoic, sterile, barren, dead: uninfluenced by life or mind.

Given the expansion of the Horizon of Contingency to cosmic catchments, it becomes *at least conceptually plausible* that we are living in that cosmic epoch before which life has spilled beyond its birthplace, so as to have a truly historic impact: perhaps to tip the wider cosmos from its currently abiotic and sterile state into something richer, more vibrant, more organic.

Yet this invites the question: has anyone else already made the attempt? Again, the anthropologist Loren Eiseley put it best in the 1950s. He wrote:

> Since we now talk ... endlessly of space rockets, it is no surprise that this thinking yields the obverse of the coin: that the rocket or its equivalent may have come first to us from somewhere 'outside'. ... Surely, in the infinite wastes of time, in the lapse of suns and wane of systems, the passage, if it were possible, would have been achieved. But the bright projectile has not been found.

Before continuing:

> Moreover, the present theory of the expanding universe has made time, as know it, no longer infinite. If the entire universe was created in a single explosive instant a few billion years ago, there has not been a sufficient period for all things to occur even behind the star shoals of the outer galaxies. In the light of this fact it is [therefore now] conceivable that there may be nowhere in space a mind superior to our own.[128]

Not many years afterward, Eiseley's question was put to empirical test. The opening of the 1960s, that is, saw the launch of the Search for Extraterrestrial Intelligence (SETI). Hopes were high that their initial searches would reveal a noisy galaxy, filled with other intelligences: perhaps more historied than us, happy to communicate the hard-won wisdoms they had learnt. Some even described this as hoped-for message as a 'short-cut to wisdom', one that may decide whether humanity survived the nuclear age or not.[129]

But SETI found nothing, only cosmic silence. Nothing, of course, has been found since. Not one sign of cosmic mind. The uneasy conclusion was swiftly reached, one which still troubles those who ponder the silent sky today. Either, something about the feat of spreading life beyond its birth planet is impossible: either materially or due to some inherent transience of 'technological intelligences' like our own. This doesn't bode well for our future. Or, hardly more comforting, we are the first, and perhaps the only, minds the universe has developed which are capable of posing such a question in the first place and worrying about what it might mean for our future. Both options, to put it lightly, are troubling.

So, where does this all leave us? To sum up, as we've learnt more about this world we've increasingly come to accept that the statements '*nature never forgets*' and '*it could all have been otherwise*' apply at increasingly titanic scales. In tandem, this has led inquirers to progressively come to appreciate the sheer contingency of everything that makes us what we are.

Not only is complex life itself the product of unrepeatable and chancy events in the ancient past: so too are all its diverse species; and, in particular, that strange lineage of life that accidentally developed sapience and science and the ability to talk in counterfactuals.

It took orienting ourselves within cosmic history as a whole to discover this most fundamental and intimate truth about what we are, where we came from, and where we might be going. Where once it was assumed we were common or inevitable, now we seem lonely, fragile, and precarious.

---

[128] Eiseley, 'Little Men and Flying Saucers'.
[129] Drake, 'On Hands and Knees in Search of Elysium'.

Each one of us is the product of an unthinkable chain of contingencies, stretching from our parents, through our shared common ancestry, to the beginning of life on Earth, and outward, potentially, to the very origins of the cosmos itself.

If any one of these contingencies had gone slightly otherwise, nothing about us would exist today. Pondering this in 1989, and imagining 'replaying the tape of life' from its beginnings, Stephen Jay Gould envisioned letting any one of our evolutionary ancestors expire. What would result? He answered:

> One little twig on the mammalian branch, a lineage with interesting possibilities that were never realized, joins the vast majority of species in extinction. So what? Most possibilities are never realized, and who will ever know the difference?

Responding to this, to modern science's teaching of the cosmic contingency of everything about *Homo sapiens*, Gould summed up his feelings:

> Make of the conclusion what you will. Some find the prospect depressing; I have always regarded it as exhilarating, and a source of both freedom and consequent moral responsibility.[130]

I agree. In a world riddled with – and *forged from* – contingency triumphant, there is room for agency meaningful action. In such a universe, there is no congenital destiny or doom. We can *make* what we are.

It also means that the disasters and crimes that are committed are not inevitable nor unavoidable. For example, the ongoing ruination of planetary ecosystems – the Sixth Mass Extinction – is not some inexorable question of fate. It is something that can go otherwise and, perhaps, the worst-case outcomes of what's already unfolding can be averted.

In a universe such as ours, one where there is no congenital destiny or doom and contingency reigns supreme, we are therefore, to borrow the resonant words of John Milton:

> Sufficient to have stood, though free to fall.

We have banished the comforts of ergodicity – wherein every possibility inevitably recurs – beyond the limits of spacetime. We must now seek these solaces and consolations in increasingly exotic, and unreachable, places: multiverses, Many Worlds Interpretations of quantum physics, cyclical cosmologies, and so forth. The degree to which have banished ergodicity outwards is the degree to which the stakes of what unfolds next have skyrocketed.

---

[130] Gould, *Wonderful Life*, p.323.

This is why the tenor and tendency of modern inquiry appears to be the revelation that what's actual is but a shrinking region within a growing kingdom of things that could have been, but simply weren't. We celebrate the discovery of Deep Space, as well as the unveiling of Deep Time, but we are yet to announce the revelation of Deep Possibility. Yet this began when the first human uttered the first counterfactual, and began building momentum after Duns Scotus offered his Medieval definition of possible worlds, before, lately, it is snowballing – with the silicon revolution and the explosion of computer simulations.

In a 1983 paper, the biologists David M. Raup and J.W. Valentine threw this all into relief. They wrote:

> Life forms are made possible by the remarkable properties of polypeptides. It has been argued that there must be many potential but unrealised polypeptides that could be used in living systems. The number of possible primary polypeptide structures with lengths comparable to those found in living systems is almost infinite. This suggests that the particular subset of polypeptides of which organisms are now composed is only one of a great many that could be associated in viable biochemistries.

Remarking that there is 'no taxonomic category available to contain all life forms descended from a single event of life origin', they proposed the term 'bioclade'. Assuming, as all the evidence indicates, that life on Earth shares one common ancestor – thus is 'monophyletic', forming one 'bioclade' – we can assume that every single organism we are familiar with occupies just one miniscule mote within an unthinkably wider space of possibility. Sounding out the proportions of that morphospace – of all possible bioclades and their splaying histories – remains a riddle for future biologists, on Earth or beyond.

Raup concluded by turning Leibniz on his head. He remarked that what is safe to conclude, for now, is that it is 'most unlikely' that 'our bioclade is the best of all possible bioclades'.[131]

Of course, Leibniz's desiderata remains: that with enough knowledge, time, or computation, we might be able to *brute force* history's complexities, so as to produce a perfect predictive model for its future. But the past teaches us that every prior generation has been reliably proven overhasty, time and again, in assuming they had come anywhere close to grasping history's entire span of possibility. The latitude of the unrealised belies our parochial tendency to assume what's actual exhausts what's possible. But, as generations before were displaced in space and time, we appear – for better or worse – to be dethroned in wider realms of

---

[131] Raup and Valentine, 'Multiple Origins'.

possibility. Perhaps this is salutary. Unpredictability has long been considered an aesthetic virtue, after all.

Grant Allen – a Canadian science writer and communicator of Darwinism – put it best, all the way back 1886:

> It is the common error of the human species to underestimate the vast and wonderful complexity of nature, [and to] overlook the whole enormous series of remote consequences that follow [upon] every act. ... Whatever we do entails far more than we ever imagined, and carries with it an entire sequence of distant effects whose very existence we never counted upon.[132]

But the fact we are *at least aware* of this limitation is one our greatest, most unique strengths. It is an achievement that can be tracked back to our ancestors who became the first to converse and conjecture in counterfactuals.

---

[132] Allen, *Common Sense Science*, p.142.

Glossary

Aretalogical – Systems of ethics which focus on expressing the virtues, of being a good person based on established habit and precedented character traits. This is contrasted with the modern systems of ethics: utilitarianism and deontology, which focus, respectively, on making the world a better place through consequential action and following rules whose legitimacy derives from their rational consistency rather than their established precedent.

Contingency – The recognition that things can be otherwise, that the ways events play out can go differently. It is the acknowledgement that something is not necessarily the way it is. When we say something is *contingent upon* something else we are harking back to Medieval discussion of the ways the world is contingent (i.e. non-necessary) such that it implies the existence of a necessary being (i.e. God, the creator).

Deep Possibility – The acknowledgement that there is far more possible than is actual and, what's more, that this may forever remain the case. Recognising this is a truth of our universe might count as an intellectual revolution comparable to the recognition Earth isn't at the centre of the universe in the 1500s and 1600s (Deep Space), and to the discovery that we are latecomers to an ancient planet in the 1700s and 1800s (Deep Time).

Diachronic possibility – A definition of possibility that tethers possibility to concrete expression within time: that is, what happens at some point in time, or, what is known to sometimes happen.

Ergodicity – The property of a system that will reliably express all of its possible states, with a 0 per cent probability of never returning to each one. Ergodic systems, given enough time, thus never exhibit history or truly irreversible change: things come, things go, but they all can always return and repeat.

Irrealis – Grammatical mood expressing situations, events, or actions that are hypothetical or unreal. Contrasted with the *realis* mood.

Modal logic – The logic behind statements of contingency, possibility, and necessity. First developed by Aristotle, modal logic now involves complicated systems of symbolic logic that express possible worlds.

Modality – The ways language can express whether something is possible, necessary, or impossible; or, in morality, whether it is permissible, obligatory, or impermissible; or, in epistemology, whether something is uncertain, true, or untrue.

Morphospace – An abstract space mapping all possible shapes or structures of an organism. It is an alluring metaphor to think of history itself having a morphospace, or, an imagined space of all possible events and outcomes. The concepts of parameter space, phase space, and state space are all similar.

Non-ergodicity – The property of a system that does *not* express all of its possible states. This means history can enter the picture, because not everything that can happen will happen, such that not all possible outcomes will come to pass regardless and therefore the influence of the past on the future can be permanent.

Ordnungschwund – Hans Blumenberg's term for the loss of an ordered, inherently rational cosmos at the beginning of the modern age: triggered by the theological need to claim God's choice in making our world was not necessitated by reason but motivated by arbitrary choice. It was stripping the universe of indwelling rational and deductive necessity that forced inquiry to develop more empirical and inductive methods.

Potentia absoluta – The late Medieval name for God's absolute, unrestricted power – that is, to have created worlds entirely unlike ours.

Potentia ordinata – The late Medieval name for God's restrained, ordered power: that is, the regularity and order he maintains within our, created world (i.e. despite the fact he could have made it entirely otherwise).

Statistical interpretation of modality – The definition of modality that assumes what is necessary is what always happens, what is possible is what sometimes happens, and what is impossible is what never happens. This was the primary, if not the sole, definition of modality until the Middle Ages.

Synchronic possibility – A definition of possibility that untethers possibility from concrete expression within time: one that conceives of possibility as simultaneous alternatives. This, importantly, acknowledges that certain possibilities don't need to ever come to pass.

Toto mundo destructo – The name for late Medieval thought experiments imagining possible worlds populated by only one, singular object. Developed as a means to show how our categorisations and impressions of the world are not necessary features of all possible worlds, and thus not themselves an inherent limit on what God can create and do.

Underdetermination – The situation when there is not yet enough evidence to choose between competing theories or models. Theory is said to be underdetermined by the evidence when it remains unclear which option, from competing alternates, is best to believe.

Voluntarism – The school of theology, prominent in both Christianity and Islam, which stresses God's free will and omnipotence. Voluntarists disagree with any claim God was in any way *compelled* to make our world the way it is, such that they are forced to argue our world, alongside its laws and all its contents, are entirely contingent.

Bibliography

Agassiz, Louis, *Iconographie des coquilles tertiaires reputees identiques avec les especes vivantes ou dans differens terrains de l'epoque tertiaire, accompagnee de la description des especes nouvelles par L. Agassiz*, Henri Wolfrath: Neuchatel, 1845.

Agassiz, Louis, and Augustus Addison Gould, *Outlines of Comparative Physiology Touching the Structure and Development of the Races of Animals, Living and Extinct*. H.G. Bohn: London, 1851.

Allen, Grant, *Common Sense Science*. Boston: Lothrop, 1886.

Alvarez, Walter, *T-Rex and the Crater of Doom*. Princeton: Princeton University Press, 1997.

Aristotle, *The Complete Works of Aristotle: The Revised Oxford Translation*, II. vols, ed. Jonathon Barnes. Princeton: Princeton University Press, 2014.

Arrhenius, Svante, *Worlds in the Making: The Evolution of the Universe*, trans. Henry Borns, New York: Harper, 1908.

Augustine, *Opera Omnia*, XVI.vols, ed. Jean-Paul Migne. Paris: Venit apud Editorem, 1841–1849.

Averroes, *Tahāfut al-tahāfut: The Incoherence of the Incoherence*, trans. Simon Van den Bergh. Oxford: Oxford University Press, 1954.

Backus, Irena, *Leibniz: Protestant Theologian*. Oxford: Oxford University Press, 2016.

Bacon, Roger, *Opus Majus*, trans. Robert Belle Burke. Philadelphia: University of Pennsylvania Press, 1928.

Ball, Robert S., 'How Long Can the Earth Sustain Life?' *Forthnightly Review*, 51 (1892), pp.478–490.

Beck, Matthias, and Beth Kewell, *Risk: A Study of Its Origins, History and Politics*. New Jersey: World Scientific, 2014.

Bernstein, Peter, *Against the Gods: The Remarkable Story of Risk*. New York: John Wiley & Sons, 1998.

Blanqui, Louis-Auguste, *Eternity by the Stars: An Astronomical Hypothesis*, trans. Frank Chouraqui. New York: Contra Mundum Press, 2013.

Borghini, Andrea, *A Critical Introduction to the Metaphysics of Modality*. London: Bloomsbury, 2016.

Brandom, Robert, *A Spirit of Trust: A Reading of Hegel's Phenomenology*. Harvard: Harvard University Press, 2019.

Brient, Elizabeth, *The Immanence of the Infinite: Hans Blumenberg and the Threshold to Modernity*. Washington, DC: Catholic University of American Press, 2002.

Browne, Thomas, *Hydriotaphia, Urn Burial, or a Discourse of the Sepulchral Urns Lately Found in Norfolk*. Hen Brome: London, 1658.

Browne, Thomas, *Posthumous Works of the Learned Thomas Browne*. Mears & Hooke: London, 1722.

Buffon, Georges, *Histoire naturelle, générale et particuliére*. XXXVI.vols. Imprimerie Royale: Paris, 1749–1789.

Cardano, Gerolamo, *The Book of My Life: De Vita Propria Liber*, trans. Jean Stoner. New York: Dutton, 1930.

Cardano, Gerolamo, *The Book on Games of Chance: The 16th Century Treatise on Probability*, trans Sydney Henry Gould. New York: Dover, 2015.

Chamberlin, Thomas Chrowder, 'Soil Wastage', *Popular Science Monthly*, 73 (1908), pp.5–12.

Cicero, *De Re Publica: Selections*, ed. James E. G. Zetzel. Cambridge: Cambridge University Press, 1995.

Cooper, Anthony Ashley (Earl of Shaftesbury), *An Inquiry Concerning Virtue, or Merit*. Manchester: Manchester University Press, 1977.

Dal Prete, Ivano, *On the Edge of Eternity: The Antiquity of the Earth in Medieval and Early Modern Europe*. Oxford: Oxford University Press, 2022.

Darwin, Charles, *On the Origin of Species by Means of Natural Selection*. John Murray: London, 1859.

Darwin, Charles, *Life and Letters of Charles Darwin*, III.vols. ed. Francis Darwin. John Murray: London, 1887.

Darwin, George, 'Radio-Activity and the Age of the Sun', *Nature*, 68 (1903), p. 496.

David, Florence Nightingale, *Games, Gods, and Gambling: A History of Probability and Statistical Ideas*. London: Charles Griffin, 1962.

de Condorcet, Nicolas, *Outlines of a Historical View of the Progress of the Human Mind*. G. Fryer & J. Franke : Baltimore, 1802.

de Maillet, Benoît, *Telliamed*, trans. Albert Victor Carozzi. Chicago: University of Illinois Press, 1968.

Devlin, Keith, *The Unfinished Game: Pascal, Fermat, and the Seventeenth-Century Letter that Made the World Modern*. New York: Basic Books, 2010.

Drake, Frank, 'On Hands and Knees in Search of Elysium', *MIT Technology Review*, 78:7 (1974), pp. 22–29.

Duhem, Pierre, *Etudes sur Léonard de Vinci*, III.vols. Paris: Hermann, 1906–1913.

Eddington, Arthur, 'The Internal Constitution of Stars', *The Observatory*, 43:557 (1920), pp. 341–358.

Eiseley, Loren, 'Is Man Alone in Space?' *Scientific American*, 189:1 (1953), pp.80–87.

Eiseley, Loren, 'Little Men and Flying Saucers', *Harper's*, 206:1234 (1954), pp.86–91.

Flammarion, Camille, *La pluralite des mondes habites*. Hachette: Paris, 1868.

Flammarion, Camille, *Astronomie populaire*. Hachette: Paris, 1888.

Freud, Sigmund, *Civilization and Its Discontents*, trans. James Strachey. New York: W. W. Norton, 1961.

Funkenstein, Amos, *Theology and the Scientific Imagination: From the Middle Ages to the Seventeenth Century*. Princeton, NJ: Princeton University Press, 1986.

Galileo, *Discoveries and Opinions of Galileo*, trans. Stillman Drake. New York: Doubleday, 1957.

Gamow, George, *Biography of the Earth*. New York: Mentor Books, 1941.

Gould, Stephen Jay, 'Sex, Drugs, Disasters, and the Extinction of the Dinosaurs', *Discover* 5:3 (1984), pp.3–6.

Gould, Stephen Jay, *Wonderful Life: The Burgess Shale and the Nature of History*. New York: Norton, 1989.

Gowland Hopkins, Frederick, 'Some Chemical Aspects of Life', *Report of the British Association for the Advancement of Science*, 103 (1933), pp.1–24.

Hacking, Ian, *The Emergence of Probability: A Philosophical Study of Early Ideas about Probability, Induction, and Statistical Inference*. Cambridge: Cambridge University Press, 1975.

Heilbroner, Robert, *Visions of the Future: The Distant Past, Yesterday, Today, and Tomorrow*. Oxford: Oxford University Press, 1996.

Hintikka, Jaako, *Time and Necessity: Studies in Aristotle's Theory of Modality*. Oxford: Oxford University Press, 1973.

Hintikka, Jaako, 'Leibniz on Plenitude, Relations, and the "Reign of Law"', in Simon Knuuttila (ed.), *Reforging the Great Chain of Being: Studies in the History of Modal Theories*. Dordrecht: Reidel, 1981, pp. 155–190.

Hippolytus, *Refutation of All Heresies*, trans. Matthew David Litwa. Atlanta: SBL Press, 2016.

Hobbes, Thomas, *Leviathan, or the Matter, Forme, & Power of a Common-Wealth Ecclesiastical and Civill*. Andrew Crooke: London, 1651.

Hutton, James, 'Theory of the Earth or an Investigation of the Laws Observable in the Composition, Dissolution, and Reparation of Land upon the Globe', *Transactions of the Royal Society of Edinburgh*, 1:2 (1788), pp.209–304.

Kapp, Karl William, *Toward a Science of Man in Society: A Positive Approach to the Integration of Social Knowledge*. The Hague: Martinus Nijhoff, 1961.

Knight, Charles, *Life through the Ages*. New York: Knopf, 1946.

Knuuttila, Simo, and Taina Holopainen, 'Conditional Will and Conditional Norms', *Synthese*, 96:1 (1993), pp.115–132.

Koestler, Arthur, 'The Boredom of Fantasy', *The Listener*, 49:1265 (1954), pp.891–893.

Koselleck, Reinhart, *Futures Past: On the Semantics of Historical Time*, trans. Keith Tribe. Massachusetts: MIT Press, 1990.

Kragh, Helge, 'The Source of Solar Energy, ca. 1840–1910: From Meteoric Hypothesis to Radioactive Speculations', *The European Physical Journal H*, 41 (2016), pp.365–394.

Kukkonen, Taneli, 'Mind and Modal Judgement: Al-Ghazālī and Ibn Rushd on Conceivability and Possibility', in Vesa Hirvonen, Toivo Holopainen, and Miira Tuominen (eds.), *Mind and Modality: Studies in the History of Philosophy in Honour of Simo Knuuttila*. Leiden: Brill, 2006. pp.121–139.

Leakey, Richard, and Roger Lewin, *The Sixth Extinction: Patterns of Life and the Future of Humankind*, New York: Anchor, 1996.

Leibniz, 'Apokatastasis panton', trans. David Forman. https://philpapers.org/rec/LEIAPA-4.

Lem, Stanisław, *One Human Minute*, trans. Catherine S. Leach. New York: Harcourt, 1986.

Lemaître, Georges, 'Evolution of the Universe', *Supplement to Nature*, 127 (1931), pp.704–706.

Lemaître, Georges, *The Primeval Atom: An Essay on Cosmogony*, trans. Betty H. Korff and Serge A. Korff, New York: Nostrand, 1950.

Lichtheim, Miriam, *Ancient Egyptian Literature*, III.vols. California: University of California Press, 1973–1980.

Lomonosov, Mikhail, *Pervyye osnovaniya metallurgii ili rudnykh del*. Saint Petersburg: Imperial Academy of Sciences, 1763.

Lucretius, *On the Nature of Things*, trans. Martin Ferguson Smith. Indianapolis: Hackett, 2001.

Machiavelli, *The Chief Works*, trans. Allan Gilbert, III.vols. North Carolina: Duke University Press, 1999.

McCabe, *The End of the World*. London: Routledge, 1920.

Miller, Stanley L., and Harold C. Urey, 'Organic Compound Synthesis on the Primitive Earth', *Science*, 130:3370 (1959), pp.245–251.

Millikan, 'When the Sun Goes Cold', *Popular Science*, 114:3 (1929), p.25, pp.140–141.

Milton, John R., 'The Origin and Development of the Concept of the "Laws of Nature"', *European Journal of Sociology*, 22:2 (1981), pp.173–195.

More, Henry, *Democritus Platonissans*. California: Clark Memorial Library, 1968.

Moynihan, Thomas, 'Existential Risk and Human Extinction: An Intellectual History', *Futures Journal*, 116 (2020).

Nicolaus de Autricuria, *The Universal Treatise of Nicholas of Autrecourt*, trans. Leonard A. Kennedy, Richard E. Arnold, and Arthur E. Millward. Milwaukee: Marquette University Press, 1971.

Oakley, Franics, 'Christian Theology and the Newtonian Science: The Rise of the Concept of the Laws of Nature', *Church History*, 30:4 (1961), pp.433–457.

Ockham, William, *Philosophical Writings*, trans. Philotheus Boehner. London: Thomas Nelson & Sons, 1957.

Ord, Toby, *The Precipice: Existential Risk and the Future of Humanity*. New York: Hachette Books, 2020.

Pascal, Blaise, *Pensées*, trans. Alban John Krailsheimer. London: Penguin, 1995.

Plato, *The Laws, Books I–IV*, trans. Robert Gregg Bury. Harvard: Harvard University Press, 1926.

Plato, *The Republic, Books VI–X*, trans. Paul Shorey. Harvard: Harvard University Press, 1935.

Plato, *Timaeus and Critias*, trans. Robin Waterfield. Oxford: Oxford University Press, 2008.

Raup, David M., and James W. Valentine, 'Multiple Origins of Life', *Proceedings of the National Academy of Sciences of the United States of America*, 80 (1983), pp.2981–2984.

Riker, Stephen, 'al-Ghazālī on Necessary Causality in "The Incoherence of the Philosophers"', *The Monist* 79:3 (1996), pp.315–324.

Rupke, Nicolaas, 'Neither Creation nor Evolution: The Third Way in Mid-Nineteenth Century Thinking about the Origin of Species', *Annals of the History & Theory of Biology* 10 (2005), pp.143–172.

Rutherford, Ernest, 'Some Cosmical Aspects of Radioactivity', *Journal of the Royal Astronomical Society of Canada*, 1:3 (1907), pp.145–165.

Saint Bonaventure, *Doctoris seraphici: Bonaventurae Opera Omnia*, X.vols. Florence: Quaracchi, 1864.

Schedel, Hartmann, *Liber Chronicarum*. Nuremberg: Koberger, 1493.

Shapley, Harlow, 'A Digression on Great Moments', *American Scholar*, 26:3 (1956), pp.354–355.

Siger of Brabant, *On the Eternity of the World*, trans. Cyril Vollert, Lottie Kendzierski, and Paul Byrne. Milwaukee: Marquette University Press, 1964.

Sol Tax, ed. *Evolution after Darwin: The University of Chicago Centennial*, III. vols. Chicago: The University of Chicago Press, 1960.

Steno, Nicolaus, *Steno: Biography & Original Papers of a 17th Century Scientist*. trans. Troels Kardel and Paul Maquet. Berlin: Springer, 2013.

Suddendorf, Thomas, Donna Addis, and Michael Corballis, 'Mental Time Travel and the Shaping of the Human Mind', *Philosophical Transanctions of the Royal Society of London B Biological Sciences*, 12:364 (2009), pp.317–1324.

Suddendorf, Thomas, Jonathan Redshaw, and Adam Bulley, *The Invention of Tomorrow: A Natural History of Foresight*. New York: Basic Books, 2022.

Thomas, Aquinas, *The Disputed Questions on Truth*, IIIvols, trans. Robert W. Mulligan. Chicago: Regnery, 1952.

Thomson, William, 'On the Mechanical Energies of the Solar System', *Transaction of the Royal Society of Edinburgh*, 21 (1854), pp.63–80.

Thucydides, *The Peloponessian War*, trans. Rex Warner, London: Penguin, 1954.

Tolkien, John Ronald Reuel, 'On Fairy-Stories', In Christopher Tolkien (Ed.), *The Monsters and the Critics, and Other Essays*. London: HarperCollins, 1990, pp.109–161.

Tyndall, John, *Heat Considered as a Mode of Motion*. London: D. Appleton & Company, 1863.

Vale, Gabriele L., Emma G. Flynn, and Rachel L. Kendal, 'Cumulative Culture and Future Thinking: Is Mental Time Travel a Prerequisite to Cumulative Cultural Evolution?' *Learning and Motivation*, 43:4 (2012), pp.220–230.

Visser, Sandra, and Thomas Williams, *Anselm*. Oxford: Oxford University Press, 2009.

Vyshedskiy, Andrey, 'Language Evolution to Revolution: The Leap from Rich-Vocabularly Non-recursive Communication System to Recursive Language 70,000 Years Ago', *Research Ideas and Outcomes*, 5 (2019). https://doi.org/10.3897/rio.5.e38546.

Weismann, August, 'Ueber die Dauer des Lebens', *Tageblatt der Versammlung deutscher Naturforscher und Aerzte in Salzburg*, 54 (1881), pp.98–114.

Wolf, Erik T., and Owen B. Toon, 'The Evolution of Habitable Climates under the Brightening Sun', *JGR Atmospheres*, 120:12 (2015), pp.5775–5794.

Young, Charles Augustus, *The Sun*. New York: D. Appleton & Company, 1881.

Cambridge Elements

Historical Theory and Practice

Daniel Woolf
Queen's University, Ontario

Daniel Woolf is Professor of History at Queen's University, where he served for ten years as Principal and Vice-Chancellor, and has held academic appointments at a number of Canadian universities. He is the author or editor of several books and articles on the history of historical thought and writing, and on early modern British intellectual history, including most recently *A Concise History of History* (CUP 2019). He is a Fellow of the Royal Historical Society, the Royal Society of Canada, and the Society of Antiquaries of London. He is married with three adult children.

Editorial Board

Dipesh Chakrabarty, *University of Chicago*
Marnie Hughes-Warrington, *University of South Australia*
Ludmilla Jordanova, *University of Durham*
Angela McCarthy, *University of Otago*
María Inés Mudrovcic, *Universidad Nacional de Comahue*
Herman Paul, *Leiden University*
Stefan Tanaka, *University of California, San Diego*
Richard Ashby Wilson, *University of Connecticut*

About the Series

Cambridge Elements in Historical Theory and Practice is a series intended for a wide range of students, scholars, and others whose interests involve engagement with the past. Topics include the theoretical, ethical, and philosophical issues involved in doing history, the interconnections between history and other disciplines and questions of method, and the application of historical knowledge to contemporary global and social issues such as climate change, reconciliation and justice, heritage, and identity politics.

Cambridge Elements

Historical Theory and Practice

Elements in the Series

Historians' Autobiographies as Historiographical Inquiry: A Global Perspective
Jaume Aurell

Historiographic Reasoning
Aviezer Tucker

Pragmatism and Historical Representation
Serge Grigoriev

History and Hermeneutics
Paul Fairfield

Testimony and Historical Knowledge: Authority, Evidence and Ethics in Historiography
Jonas Ahlskog

Race, Genetics, History: New Practices, New Approaches
Alexandra P. Alberda, Njabulo Chipangura, Lara Choksey, Jerome de Groot, Maya Sharma

Contested Public Monuments: Global perspectives on landscapes of memory
Maria Grever

Gender, Theory, and History: On the Knowledge and Politics of Bodies
María Inés La Greca

Things of the Past: A Modern Yearning
Kasper Risbjerg Eskildsen

Myths, History Wars, and Indigenous–Settler Reconciliation in Canada and Other Settler States
David Bruce Amichand MacDonald

Knowledge and Narrative
Chiel van de Akker

The History of Contingency and Future-Oriented Thought
Thomas Moynihan

A full series listing is available at: www.cambridge.org/EHTP